TALES WITHOUT REASON

Fr Thomas O'Malley CSSp

Tales Without Reason

FORGOTTEN HEROES OF THE APOSTOLATE IN 1840s AUSTRALIA

the columba press

First published in 2001 by
the columba press
55A Spruce Avenue, Stillorgan Industrial Park,
Blackrock, Co Dublin

Cover by Bill Bolger
Origination by The Columba Press
Printed in Ireland by Colour Books Ltd, Dublin

ISBN 1 85607 336 X

Contents

Preface

Against the backdrop of colonial imperialism in the South Pacific and relentless competition between the British and the French in the early 19th century, this book paints a finite, human picture. It is the story of a handful of men and women whose spiritual sights were set on the remote and little-known continent of Australia, where, they believed, their missionary efforts would bring the salvation of faith and civilisation.

Perth and Albany, both founded as penal colonies in Western Australia in the late 1820s, remained isolated outposts accessible only by sea until 1841. John Brady, consecrated Bishop of Perth in 1845, set out to recruit European missionaries to minister to the purported two million natives in the surrounding area. In July 1845 he met with Father Francis Libermann, Superior General of the newly founded Missionaries of the Holy Heart of Mary, at La Neuville (Amiens) and secured the services of Father François Thévaux and Father François-Joseph Thiersé. Two months later Brady and his band of 27 missionaries set sail from London.

Like any adventure that involves a complex cast of characters, *Tales Without Reason* is a story of personalities, ambitions, and often conflicting visions: Libermann, after setbacks and disillusionment in Haiti and Guinea (West Africa), is eager to establish missions that will demonstrate the efficacy of his young Congregation; Thévaux and Thiersé, both newly ordained and also young (Thiersé was 31 and Thévaux just 26), are obedient to Libermann but also compelled to make the most of this unusual opportunity; and Brady, while his motives are rarely clear or his actions straightforward, seems driven to make a name for himself in the emerging colony. From these men's letters and the observations of other key players, we see the distance that often arises between authority and responsibility, idealism and reality.

While there is no shortage of physical hardship here – which we should expect of the time and place in which this story unfolds – *Tales Without Reason* has more to do with the moral privation that can result when spiritual agendas collide.

Thomas Grizzard

Introduction

There is a history in all men's lives.
— *Henry IV, Part 2, Act III, i*

My very dear Father,
I intend in this letter to give you a full report of everything that has happened in the Mission to which you sent us, starting from the very moment of our arrival here.[1]

Thus begins the report of Father François M. Thévaux on the Mission of King George Sound, New Holland (Australia), 1846-1848. It was addressed to Father Francis Mary Paul Libermann, Superior General of the newly founded 'Missionaries of the Holy Heart of Mary,' at La Neuville, Amiens, France. It is a story of atrocious suffering heroically borne, and one which has gone largely unnoticed.

While the story of the first Catholic mission in Western Australia may not be one of the great events of the Congregation of the Holy Spirit, it is a human story textured with hopes and joys and sorrows, and worthy of great compassion and admiration. It began in July 1845, when Venerable Father Libermann received at La Neuville a four-day visit from the Irishman, John Brady, newly consecrated Bishop of Perth, Australia. The two men had little in common except proven devotion to the apostolate.

Though Libermann had been ordained just four years earlier, in 1841, several of his missionaries were already in the field. Blessed Jacques Laval was in Mauritius, Indian Ocean, where he worked alone because the British Government did not favour the presence of French missionaries in their former colony. Father Frederic Le Vavasseur was in a somewhat better – if also politically precarious – position in Bourbon (Réunion Island), 200 miles southwest of Mauritius.[2]

PART I

Libermann's Dilemma

On 27 March 1840, Libermann had presented a memorandum to the Congregation for the Propagation of the Faith (*Propaganda Fide*), a plan for the evangelisation of the blacks composed by himself and the two other co-founders of the Society of the Holy Heart of Mary, Frederic Le Vavasseur and Eugene Tisserant. Their original foray was to take place in Haiti, the first Black Republic.

In August 1843, Fr Tisserant arrived in Haiti to launch the new Mission. In 1844 he was named Prefect Apostolic, but by February 1845 new authorities showed open hostility, and Tisserant felt it necessary to leave the country for good. At the beginning of May 1845 he returned to France with his whole team.[3]

Seven of Libermann's very first missionaries had set out in 1843 for the Two Guineas, an area stretching 5,000 miles along the West African coast with no limit into the interior. Within a year all were reported dead and only two actually survived that inhospitable coast.[4] By 1845 a mission to Dakar had succeeded, but with their missionary approach Libermann's men were an unwelcome intrusion, and the colonial priests, who were primarily chaplains to the white and mulatto populations, looked askance at these missionaries who wished to devote themselves to the conversion of the infidels.

It became clear to Libermann that the uncertainty and the urgency of the situation were putting the very future of his Congregation at risk. On 20 March 1846 he reflected:

Our congregation was beginning to prosper, the candidates were coming along; it was urgent for us to have a Mission, an important one to show. We were becoming known in the dioceses of France when all of a sudden we were without a Mission – none in the colonies and almost none in Guinea. This would have had quite a bad effect: our people would have been discouraged, our good name in the dioceses would have suffered, we would have gone backwards. And be sure that it is very hard to set up anew an undertaking which falls backward after a promising start…[5]

In several letters from this period he returned to the same theme: 'Our Mission to the natives is a mission of patience… In the meantime we have to have a solid starting point, an important Mission. Without this we risk losing the esteem of the French clergy.'[6]

In the summer of 1845, Brady's visit at La Neuville opened the door to a timely opportunity: the prospect of establishing the fledgling Congregation's first outpost in the vast continent of Australia:

…while this is going on, Propaganda in Rome is sending us a bishop from New Holland and commends his mission to us. That is exactly what was needed: a vast mission, comprising several million savage heathens. We had missionaries ready to be used. If not accepted I would not have known where to employ them; they were impatient and half discouraged by not having a job to do…[7]

His colleagues at La Neuville were unanimous in their support,[8] but he knew that the decision would arouse a storm of objections among his men already in the field. Seeking to calm matters, he explained why the decision was taken and replied patiently but firmly to the letters of protest he received:

I believe it is prudent and according to the divine will that we accept another Mission which was recommended to us by Propaganda, which is fine with us. It is the Australian or New Holland Mission. It is important for us now to be able to present a stable Mission… You will all cry: 'Why don't you send us that excess of manpower,' and I will answer you: 'but where would you find the means to live?' The Australian

Mission will, I hope, bring more people than it will take away from us.[9]

And to Fr Arragon in Senegal, who harangued him with recriminatory letters, he wrote:

You got it into your head and keep on repeating that this new Mission means losing the Guinea Mission. I have told you, I repeat again and I will always repeat that Guinea will be our first Mission and that we would take the utmost care of it. If I were to send ten missionaries to Guinea instead of the seven you have there, would you do more with them at this time? Could you employ them? So let me get on with it: the general administration of the congregation has been entrusted to me. As for you, you don't have the *grace d'etat* for that.[10]

The scene was now set for the four-day visit of Bishop Brady at La Neuville.

Bishop Brady's Early Career in Australia

John Brady was born in 1789 in County Cavan, Ireland[11], and studied for the priesthood at the Holy Ghost Seminary in Paris.[12] After ordination Brady volunteered for work in Bourbon, where he won the highest praise for his priestly zeal.

In 1836 he returned to Europe after falling out with Father Poncelet, the Prefect Apostolic, complaining about the way in which he had been treated. Father Poncelet's authoritarian manner had alienated him from most of his priests, but with Father Brady things seem to have gone further. On 22 February 1837 Father Fourdinier, Superior General of the Holy Ghost Fathers, wrote to the Cardinal Prefect of Propaganda:

He (Father Brady) carries many testimonials about with him from the most eminent citizens of the parishes where he exercised the sacred ministry... Until the coming of Father Poncelet we had none but good testimonies about his conduct, and now Father Poncelet writes against him in the strongest terms: he accuses him of avarice, of injustice, of hypocrisy, and of a perfidious wickedness... This seems quite exaggerated... He has doubtless made serious mistakes since Father Poncelet treated him severely, but I am loath to believe that he is as bad as he is made out to be.[13]

In Rome that same year Father Brady met Dr Ullathorne OSB, Vicar General of New Holland (now Australia), which – like Capetown, Madagascar, New Zealand and Tasmania – at that time came under the ecclesiastical jurisdiction of the Bishop of Port Louis, Mauritius.

Brady now volunteered for service in New South Wales. He arrived in Sydney in 1838 and was appointed first to the notorious penal colony of Norfolk Island, 1,000 miles northeast of Sydney, and later to the district of Windsor, New South Wales. He was highly admired as a staunch defender of convicts. He also became interested in the aborigines and claimed to have written a dictionary of their language. A controversial character, he successfully sued two Sydney papers for libel and put them out of business.

In 1834 Rome had appointed John Bede Polding OSB of Downside Abbey as Vicar Apostolic of New Holland (Australia), Van Diemen's Land (Tasmania), and the islands of Madagascar and New Zealand – a vast area now to be separated from the jurisdiction of Mauritius. Polding soon discovered that it was impossible to administer Perth (the Swan River Colony) in Western Australia because of its remote location. On 1 September 1843 he appointed Fr Brady as his Vicar General, and by early October Brady had arrived in Adelaide on his way to Albany on King George Sound. Included in his party were Patrick O'Reilly, an Irish catechist, and Fr John Joostens, a Belgian and one-time chaplain in Napoleon's army.

Their arrival in Adelaide was welcomed by the town's solitary priest, a Father Benson, who had seen a brother priest only once in his three years in South Australia. They waited with him for some time before they were able to get a ship sailing westward. Finally on 4 November 1843 they arrived at Albany, a small whaling station situated on the southern slopes of Mount Clarence and Mount Melville.

Albany

Albany was a port of call for many whaling nations. Hence it sometimes happened that ships' chaplains would come ashore to say Mass, an opportunity seldom afforded the few local Catholics. We read of the resident magistrate, Sir Richard Spencer, writing to the Colonial Secretary in Perth in 1838:

> On 18 January, the French Frigate, *Heroine*, Captain Cecille, anchored in the Sound for the protection of French whalers on this coast, and on the 11th the French whaler *Harmonie* anchored, and remained five weeks, when she sailed to Two People Bay. She had 1,200 Barrels of oil in.[14]

There is little doubt that the French frigate carried a chaplain, and that he landed and said Mass for the sailors, for the whalers, and for the few Catholics. Mrs A.Y. Hassel writes in her 'Early Memories of Albany,' published in 1917:

> I am sorry that I have not been able to get the exact date the first Roman Catholic priest arrived in Albany, because it was an interesting event. A vessel anchored at Albany, and on board a French priest, who, on landing, found there members of his flock, so an open service was held on the side of the hill just above the Deep Water Jetty, and the first Mass was said within the shadow of the two round rocks one on top of the other at the corner off Brunswick Road. This occurred some time towards the end of the thirties.[15]

Fr Brady and his party celebrated Mass at this hallowed place and went on to baptise the children of one Lawrence Mooney, an Irish ex-soldier of the 21st Regiment of Foot. Born in 1809, he received his army discharge in Albany in 1840. Today these rocks carry a bronze plaque with the inscription:

> *At these Rocks in January 1838 Holy Mass was celebrated for the first time in the settlement of Western Australia. The Chaplain of the French Frigate the Heroine gathered the few Catholics of Frederickstown [Albany's original name] to this place and offered Mass. The Albany Port Authority, in Albany's Sesquicentenary year (1977) erected this plaque to mark the site where Catholic worship in Western Australia first began. 20th March 1977*

As an old man, in 1887, Lawrence Mooney told Cardinal Moran of his sorrow at not being able to hear Mass:

> He was accustomed on Sundays to climb to the summit of Mount Clarence, reciting the rosary and shedding bitter tears at the thought that there was not a priest, or altar, or Holy Sacrifice within a thousand miles of him; and turning towards the west he would unite in spirit with his distant countrymen, and pray fervently to God that he might not be left always in desolation.[16]

Fr Brady and his party could not stay long, and on board the *Water Witch* they continued on to Fremantle, at the mouth of the Swan River, arriving there on 8 December 1843.

The Swan River Colony

Fremantle and Perth on the Swan River were both founded in 1829. At the time of Fr Brady's arrival the population was reckoned to be about 3,000, under the control of Governor Hutt. The Catholic population was difficult to estimate, but one of the Sisters of Mercy estimated that in 1845 there were perhaps 30 in Perth. Dr Richard Madden, the first Catholic Colonial Secretary, estimated that in 1847 there were not 90 Catholics within a 10-mile radius of Perth. According to the government *Gazette* of 19 December 1848, the total number of Catholics in the whole of Western Australia amounted to only 337 persons. Governor Hutt received Fr Brady cordially and gave him three allotments of land on which to build a church, school, and presbytery, and he promised a liberal subscription.

Father Brady Goes to Rome

The building of a church was begun on the 27th of December and dedicated to St John the Evangelist, whose feast day it was; the foundation stone was laid on 16 January 1844. Father Brady's flock, with few exceptions, was of the poorest class, but even non-Catholics gave generously. 'In a few hours a subscription of £160 was handed in, auguring well for the future.'[17]

After a short time, having made some visits to outlying areas, Brady decided to go to Europe for financial support and to recruit missionaries. Without any reference to his superior, Archbishop Polding, he sailed on 11 February 1844 to Batavia, Dutch East Indies, heading for Rome on board the *Ganges*. Fr Joostens, left behind as Vicar General, organised a school in the incomplete church.[18]

In Rome Fr Brady strongly advocated that a diocese should be erected in Perth with its own Bishop, with two distinct missions to be established for the aborigines: one at King George Sound and another in the north of Australia at Port Essington (Darwin). His proposal was presented only to the weekly meeting of the Propaganda Office, which rejected it.

Grievously disappointed, as he was preparing to leave the city he met Bishop Luguet, a famous and influential missionary. Well ahead of his time, Luguet had argued for the ordination of local bishops and priests as the sure basis for a local church. Bishop Luguet chided Brady for his discouragement and pledged to present a memorandum on his behalf to the Cardinals of the Congregation of the Propagation of the Faith (Propaganda). Moreover, he helped the young missionary prepare the document. The Cardinals were deeply impressed, and Brady was duly appointed Bishop of Perth and Vicar Apostolic of the Sound and of Port Essington.[19]

In a letter to Propaganda dated 31 October 1844, Brady claimed that

> There are in Perth and its district about 5,000 of white population and 2 million blacks. In the other districts the European population is but scattered, but the blacks are very numerous, being estimated at two millions. The aborigines are far superior to those of New South Wales; they are of dark olive colour and have long hair. The Government and the white population are most anxious to civilise them and to show some kindness to them.[20]

He went on to say that the aborigines took a great liking to himself and expressed their joy in a thousand ways when he told them that he came in the name of the Good Spirit, whom they called *Wangaul* (or *Wagyl*), to save them and their children from the evil spirit.

Consecration of Bishop Brady

The consecration of Fr Brady took place in the Collegiate Church of Propaganda, 18 May 1845, without any consultation with his bishop, Dr Polding of Sydney! The latter was astonished. Polding had approved Brady's departure for Europe in a letter of 23 March 1845 (well after the fact), but it makes no mention of establishing a new jurisdiction in Australia. Unless there is proof to the contrary, one cannot doubt the authenticity of this letter, even though there were rumours that Brady was elected bishop on the basis of a letter he himself had composed.[21]

On 22 February 1845 Father Brady had written a statement for *Propaganda* outlining the forsaken condition of Catholics in Western Australia. In a strange postscript, he added that if Rome nominated a bishop or an apostolic vicar, the consecration should take place in Europe and not in Sydney. The great distance between Sydney and Perth, and the scarcity of ships on that route would delay the establishment of a mission by two years. Besides, there was no need to fear the Archbishop, who had already given Brady *carte blanche* with regard to the missions. But Brady, '…not trusting his own judgement, awaited these nominations from the wisdom of the Sacred Congregation alone.'[22]

While Bishop Polding admired the zeal of Father Brady, he did not regard him as episcopal material because of his lack of discretion. Those who knew Brady would agree. Even Ullathorne was taken aback. Nonetheless, Polding accepted Brady's appointment and promised to help him in any way possible.

His Missionary Band

In Rome Brady began recruiting his missionary band. Cardinal Fransoni put him in touch with two Spanish Benedictine monks of St Martin of Compostella, Joseph Benedict Serra and Rosendo Salvado, who had left their country because of religious persecution. They were now settled in La Cava, in southern Italy. Both were gifted men who volunteered for Brady's mission and would contribute immensely to the church in Western Australia.[23]

Two additional recruits were also added: Nicolas Caporelli, a young Italian teacher destined for the proposed Diocesan College, and Father Angelo Confalonieri, born in the Italian Tyrol and educated in the College of Propaganda in Rome. Confalonieri's extant letters record the following details:

To give your Excellency before quitting Europe some account of myself and my party is a duty imposed by gratitude, respect and love, which your excellent heart encourages me to discharge. First of all, however, permit me to renew the thanks, which my Benedictine companions Serra and Salvado have already conveyed, for the hundred francs paid to me by Monsignor Fornari, Nuncio in Paris. God will repay it to you abundantly in heaven. The health of our whole party and our journey has been blessed by Providence, and we all arrived in London. At Lyon (June 15th) we remained seven days in the house of the Marist Fathers, and we had good success with the Society of the Propagation of the Faith (a voluntary Society of moral and financial support for the missions). A sum of 40,000 francs has been allotted to our mission, of which 28,000 has been paid already and the rest will soon be forwarded.

At Paris we were obliged to remain for almost a month to arrange matters with the Society of the Propagation of the Faith, and to provide things for our future mission. The Benedictine Abbot (Dom Prosper Gueranger, the famous liturgist) gave us a theological student (Léandre Fonteinne), an excellent youth. At Amiens, Providence proved most favourable to us, for Father Libermann, Superior of the priests of the Holy Heart of Mary, supplied our mission with three young priests and two lay Brothers. Also in London the visit of our bishop to the Prime Minister appears to have been favourable to the mission. I remained for a whole month in Dublin, where I enjoyed the society of my dear friend, Dr Doyle. The bishop in the meantime was in search of missionaries, but I know not why … he was able to secure only some students, all in rhetoric, though of strong constitution and over twenty years of age, besides one priest. Also six nuns from Dublin, of the Order of Mercy.[24]

Brady's Agreement with Father Libermann
Father Libermann had established the first house of the newly founded Society of the Holy Heart of Mary at La Neuville, Amiens. (In 1848 this brotherhood would be joined to the Society of the Holy Ghost Fathers to form the Congregation of the Holy Ghost and the Holy Heart of Mary.) Bishop Brady was not the first Irishman to call on the fledgling missionary order. In May 1842, John Hand, founder of The Missionary College of All Hallows, Dublin, had come to La Neuville just as Libermann was in need of British subjects to serve as missionaries in Mauritius.[25]

Now, in 1845, it was Brady who needed manpower, and he had come to Libermann in search of it. The Bishop placed before the Venerable Father the needs of his Mission and his hopes for the future, promising to give Libermann's missionaries one of the two vicariates of his Mission. Libermann convened the members of his community and all voted unanimously for acceptance.[26] How could they have done otherwise, given Brady's version of the situation in Western Australia? The missionary magazine *L'Ami de la Religion* of 10 July 1845 gives us a sample:

This prelate whose diocese extends over more than 800 leagues has neither a church nor a bishopric. Everything remains to be created in this distant land where religion has not yet spread its divine light. More than 2,000,000 savages form part of the immense flock of Bishop Brady. He has lived in the bush with these people so far removed from civilisation. This intrepid missionary was happy among them… Crowds of them approached the black robe and received joyfully and gratefully the words of peace and of consolation with which he addressed them. Quite secure amidst these savages he applied himself to the study of their language, producing a dic-

tionary which has just been printed by Propaganda [of which
no trace remains]. The zeal and the virtues of Bishop Brady
so impressed them that when he was about to leave them to
come to Europe, they could not stop repeating: 'Come back,
come back soon among us to teach us to know and love God.
Oh, when shall we see black robes stay and remain with
us!'[27]

About the same time, Brady sent a circular to all the bishops of
France asking for priests: 'My Mission comprises two million infidels over and above those in the interior whose numbers still
probably cannot be known.' In the *L'Ami de la Religion* it was reported that: 'Even though they are divided into tribes and have
chieftains, they are nearly always in a state of war or extermina-
tion.' In the circular to the bishops, on the contrary: '… each tribe
has its king and lives in mutual understanding with his neighbours.'

The circular concludes:

To those priests who wish to come to my Mission, I would
advise them to join forces with the community of missionaries called the Holy Heart of Mary, of the diocese of Amiens,
where they will find all the desirable guarantees for the
maintenance of piety and full security for the future in the
event of infirmity. The applications that are made after my
departure have to be addressed to the Superior of the missionaries at La Neuville, near Amiens.[28]

(There is no evidence of any response and no trace of the circular
in Libermann's correspondence.)

There is no document setting out the conditions on which the
agreement was made with Bishop Brady. Libermann later stated
that it was verbal, and his letter to Cardinal Franzoni dated 11
October 1845 is quite clear: 'The Holy Bishop is to confide one of
the two vicariates attached to his diocese to our missionaries.
There they will exercise their ministry under his authority.'[29]

Libermann wrote a similar letter (dated 14 October 1845) to
the Secretary of the Society of the Propagation of the Faith at
Lyon. Two additional letters (the first of 1 March 1847 to the

Cardinal Prefect, and another of 15 June 1847 to François Le
Vavasseur) imply there had been an agreement.[30] To Le
Vavasseur, for example, he wrote: 'If Bishop Brady had been
willing to adhere to the terms on which we had agreed...' In a
letter of 28 January 1846 he is more explicit: 'I am of your opinion that we ourselves should be in charge of our mission... Also,
when I treated with the Bishop of Perth, Australia, it was on condition that our missionaries should be in charge of one of the
two vicariates attached to his Mission ...later when it pleases
God to bless that Mission, the vicariate would be erected into a
diocese.'[31]

Brady's Bombshell

When he departed from La Neuville, Bishop Brady left a letter
for Libermann. It was Brady's habit to deliver at the last moment
letters that seemed to cast doubt on what had been agreed beforehand. We do not have this note which disturbed the
Venerable Father so much, but we do have his reply, dated 23
July 1845; it concerned a crucial point: the powers of the bishop
over the missionaries.

> It is understood that you are absolute master in your
> Mission, and that the missionaries will be entirely subject to
> you. It is for us an absolute rule to obey the ecclesiastical su-
> periors of the Missions that employ us, as we would obey the
> diocesan bishops in Europe.[32]

The Venerable Father seems to fear two things: first, that his
missionaries in their apostolic work might report to someone
other than the bishop; and second, that the bishop might inter-
fere in the internal affairs of the communities and give orders
contrary to the rule. 'I am not asking that the vicariate where
they are stationed should be set up as an independent bishopric... We are not asking to be masters of the Missions where
we are employed, but solely to be able to work for the salvation
of souls with all the holy freedom of the apostolic ministry
under the authority of the legitimate heads.' Having mentioned
the existence of the rules of the small Congregation, Father

Libermann elaborates:

> You [Brady] are the absolute master in everything concern-
> ing the external ministry of our missionaries. They owe you
> perfect obedience and a precise account of everything they
> do. The internal affairs of the community must be directed by
> its Superior. For if missionary bishops were to regulate the
> conduct of the missionaries within their community, our
> communities would be vulnerable and moreover there
> would no longer be any uniformity throughout the various
> communities, which would be gravely wrong... What we are
> requiring is that the ecclesiastical superiors should not take
> part of our rule away. We request that our Lord Bishops not
> ask our missionaries anything contrary to our rules. These
> rules are:
>
> – evangelical poverty;
> – obedience and submission to the superiors of the
>   Community;
> – that the missionaries should not work for any length of
>   time in isolation or alone.
>
> The spirit of our rules is as follows: a spirit of poverty, of obe-
> dience, of internal mortification, of the simplicity of minister-
> ing to the poor, and a spirit of community life.
>
> Our Lord Bishops have every authority over our missionar-
> ies; but we are asking them not to give direct assignments to
> individual missionaries without previous reference to the
> Superiors, the head of the station, and they can be certain of
> his perfect obedience. It is easy to imagine the great disorder
> that would take place in a community if individual mission-
> aries were in direct relationship of obedience to the Lord
> Bishops.[33]

This marks the first serious and concrete effort to reconcile the
powers of the ecclesiastical authority with the powers of the
religious Superior. The Venerable Libermann himself, and especially his successor, Father Schwindenhammer, were to experience painful confrontations with Vicars-Apostolic who were

themselves members of the Congregation. An attempt would be made to evade this problem by combining in one person the functions of Vicar-Apostolic and the religious Superior. But only since the Second World War has a satisfactory manner of operating been achieved.[34]

On 28 January 1846, still unaware of all the difficulties that were to arise in Australia, Libermann wrote:

> I share your opinion that we ourselves should be in charge of our Missions. Accordingly, when I was dealing with the Bishop of Perth in Australia, it was under the express condition that our missionaries should be in charge of one of the two vicariates attached to his Mission, and that they be in sole charge, except for giving him an account of their work. Later on, when God will be pleased to bless this Mission, the Vicariate would be raised to the rank of Diocese. If we then have a man worthy of the episcopate and capable of managing its affairs, it will be one of our own; otherwise I will see to it that there is a delay in naming a bishop.[35]

Here we find an unequivocal expression of the policy that Libermann had communicated more diplomatically in his letter to Brady (cited above).

Brady was quick to reply to that letter, and he apologised for having given Libermann the trouble of explaining the rules of the Society of the Holy Heart of Mary. These '…are so good and so appropriate for stirring up the apostolic spirit that I wish all my missionaries were guided by them.' He considered himself fortunate to have houses of the Holy Heart of Mary in all the territories under his jurisdiction:

> The internal discipline (of the communities) is not a matter of concern to bishops or superiors (ecclesiastical) of the Missions. In sending you my little note, I tried only to tell the current position, or rather the connection of the two with the See of Perth, the Holy See having ruled thus for wise and prudent reasons. Later on, we hope to make other arrangements, about which you will certainly be advised and consulted. In the meanwhile, you may count on me for the place-

ment of the good Missionary Fathers whom you are good
enough to entrust to me.[36]

Regarding these negotiations and clarifications of authority,
Littner observes:

> Bearing in mind this letter and what was to happen later, I
> believe that the notorious letter of Bishop Brady specified a
> point which had not been touched on in the negotiations. He
> repeated that the missionaries of the Holy Heart of Mary
> would have one of the two vicariates. But he had not dared to
> say directly that for grave reasons of prudence the Holy See
> had entrusted the Bishop of Perth with these two vicariates
> so as not to raise difficulties with the British authorities, no
> British subject having been found to fulfil the functions of
> Vicar-Apostolic. Bishop Brady would not therefore be able to
> entrust the position of chief of the mission of the vicariate to a
> Father of the Holy Heart of Mary, as they were French na-
> tionals, but would have to appoint one of the Irish priests he
> was hoping to find.[37]

Later on, since the law required two years of residence for obtaining British nationality, Brady would be able to make other
arrangements. It is this presence of a non-member of the
Congregation as head of the Mission that Libermann would ob-
ject to, and later on so would his missionaries. Today all this is
clear, but in 1845 the guidelines were imprecise and ill-defined.
It was hard to see how any third person could act as intermedi-
ary between the bishop and the group of missionaries. That is
where all the misunderstanding lay.[38]

The decision had thus been made: a group of missionaries of
the Holy Heart of Mary was to go to Australia. In August
Libermann mentions Fathers Thévaux, Bouchet, and Acker, and
the Brothers Odon and Eusäbe in his letters.[39]

Libermann's Men

Fr François Thévaux 1820–1877

François Thévaux was born of humble and pious parents at Parent, the Diocese of Clermont (Puy-de-Dome), on 15 August 1820. At ten years of age François went to school to the parish priest of St Babel. From early on he was remarkable for his piety and generosity, and he began his clerical studies at the junior seminary of Billom.

In October 1839 he entered the major seminary of Clermont. Some of his notes from this period reveal striking aspirations:

> Consider, Oh! My soul, that the seminary is uniquely for the children of the sanctuary. Consider how right and pure should be the intentions of those who enter here. Tremble and hasten to reform your outlook, if you came here only with the intention of enriching your family, and gaining the esteem of distinguished men of the world. I try to purify my intentions, not to have any other view but the glory of God and His greatest glory. Everything for my good Lord.[40]

From the first year in the seminary, with the consent of his spiritual director, he made a private vow of chastity. This was on 12 July 1840, the feast of the Sacred Heart of Jesus in his diocese. In his notes he recorded it as one of the most wonderful days of his life.

Thévaux's desire for sanctification extended to his family. To one of his brothers who joined the army, he sent a notebook full of practical spiritual advice. And from time to time throughout his life he continued this apostolate to his family. In a letter to his parents he reminds them:

...I desire the salvation of you all. I wish you all in paradise where I hope we enter through the infinite merits of our Saviour, Jesus Christ. In the seminary I could save myself with ease; you others have not much help for this. These are the considerations which lead me to give you some advice without your being annoyed with me. The good God has given me good parents. Oh! If they are fervent Christians, nothing less will make me happy.[41]

While he was at Clermont seminary, run by the Sulpicians, he met Father Gamon, one of the directors, who was also a devoted friend of Libermann. Through Gamon, especially, he got to know the 'Work for the Blacks.' Together with a fellow student, Lossedat, Thévaux decided to apply to Libermann for admission to the Work. On 12 February 1843 Libermann replied in a long letter in which he summarises three points:

If you learn the three things I wish to suggest to you, the effort you make to read my long letter will be worthwhile. Such as, firstly, forget your own concerns and the love of suffering; submit to the will of God in all trials. Secondly, always humble yourself before the Lord; have a humble opinion of your self and be aware of your nothingness; but let your humility be peaceful, gentle and full of confidence and love. Thirdly, as for the interior life, abandon yourself to Our Saviour without struggle, without any violent effort or overstraining.[42]

It wasn't until the following year, on the Feast of St Joseph (19 March 1844), that Thévaux could be admitted to the noviciate at La Neuville as a deacon. In September he was ordained and at age 24 made his consecration to the apostolate. His noviciate was cut short because of the urgent demand for missionaries, and soon after Bishop Brady's visit Thévaux departed for Australia. He was appointed Superior of the band of Libermann's five men who sailed with Brady from Gravesend, London, on 17 September 1845.

Fr Louis Acker 1813–?
Acker was born on 23 February 1813, entered the noviciate in

1843, and was ordained on 24 December 1844. He was an unexceptional man who knew small success in any job he had. He obstinately refused his nomination to the Australian mission. Father Thévaux went to see him, begging him to accept. Father Acker insulted him to the extent that '...the screams of Father Acker and sobs of Father Thévaux (as on returning to his room he wept aloud) were heard in nearby rooms.'[43]

Later he likewise refused to go to Guinea, preferring to return to his diocese of Strasbourg, thus avoiding a formal dismissal. He became parish priest of Eberbach in Alsace.

Fr François-Joseph Thiersé 1815–1880

As a replacement for Acker, Libermann chose François-Joseph Thiersé. He was born 7 June 1815 at Hochfelden in Alsace (Lower Rhine), in the diocese of Strasbourg. His father had been sentenced to death in 1793 by the notorious apostate monk, Schneider, for sheltering a rebel priest, but he fled for his life and returned home in 1802.

Up to the age of 22 François-Joseph worked on the family farm. He considered settling down to that life, but suddenly decided to become a priest. 'To work on this miserable land forever, what a life!'[44] He promptly made his resolution known to his parish priest, and eight days later broke off his projected marriage and commenced the study of Latin and Greek under the priest's tuition.

He received the Diaconate in June 1844, just as Father Schwindenhammer came to the seminary seeking recruits for Libermann's new missionary body. It was the first opportunity for the young man to hear of this apostolic vocation, and he did not resolve to join until later that summer. On April 15 the following year, Thiersé turned up at Amiens, accompanied by his younger brother, Jean-Baptiste, who also desired to join the same society. François-Joseph was ordained on 24 August 1845 and in September sailed from Gravesend with Bishop Brady's party.

Fr Maurice Bouchet 1821–1846

Father Maurice was born 7 June 1821 at Villy-le-Bauveret, dio-
cese of Annecy. Maurice did his ecclesiastical studies at St
Sulpice Seminary and joined the diocese of Paris. On 28 May
1844 he entered the noviciate of the Holy Heart of Mary, La
Neuville, and made his apostolic consecration on 21 November
the same year. His first mission appointment was to Haiti in
February 1845. He accompanied the recently appointed Prefect
Apostolic, Eugene Tisserant, who with Libermann was one of
the founders of the Work of the Blacks, the Society of the Holy
Heart of Mary.

Returning from Haiti with the other members of that failed
mission, Bouchet found himself en route to Western Australia
with his confrères Thévaux, Thiersé, and two lay brothers,
Brother Vincent Eusäbe and Brother Théodore Odon.

Brother Théodore Odon 1825–?

Born in Bordeaux in 1825, Odon took vows at the same time as
Thiersé, on 8 September 1845. Shortly after his arrival in Perth he
asked to be released from his vows. He stayed on in the city,
working as a shoemaker for Bishop Brady's seminarists, and
eventually he left the colony for South Africa.

Brother Vincent Eusäbe 1824–?

Eusäbe was also born in Bordeaux, in 1824, and like Brother
Odon he came from the orphanage there. At the age of 20 he entered the noviciate at La Neuville, Amiens, and by May 1845 he
joined the group sailing for Australia – to the surprise of everyone and especially Father Libermann. Writing to Father Clair,
director of the brothers, Libermann recorded:

> Brother Vincent left La Neuville, and did so with a minimum
> of preparation and publicity. I am nonetheless not worried
> about him: he is such a pious young man! He was fearful of
> being drafted into the army and left to safeguard himself.
> One fine day he came to see me, dressed in his Sunday
> clothes, a package under his arm, telling me he was leaving
> and that he was coming to say good- bye. He seemed happy

and at peace. He told me: 'I can see that later on I shall be forced to leave; all the same, I prefer to go right away.' [45]

After his visit with Libermann, Brady and his party left for London via Boulogne, arriving on 31 July 1845. Brady, Confalonieri, and Caporelli continued on to Dublin to seek reinforcements. The three Benedictines – Serra, Salvado and Fonteinne – went to visit their fellow Benedictines in Downside Abbey, 112 miles from London. While in Dublin, Bishop Brady wrote a letter dated 27 August, promising:

I will take care of everything for the trip, except for cassocks and surplices, and altar linen. As for church ornaments, I have enough for three Missions. They may bring a missal, a breviary, a Gradual and a Vesperal for each priest and Graduals and Vesperals for the student-catechists. If you can find pictures and paintings and altar linen etc., don't hesitate to send them. As for the cassocks, shirts, etc. for the missionaries and the catechists, we shall find them in London.[46]

The Mercy Convent, Baggot Street, Dublin

In Dublin Bishop Brady was introduced to the Irish Sisters of Mercy (Baggot Street) by a Father J. Smyth, who later became the bishop's agent or Procurator. Smyth was a man held in high esteem by the nuns. The Superior of their order, Mother Cecilia Marmion, listened to the bishop's picture of the Perth scene, with its seven schools and 4,000 children 'with no one to break for them the bread of instruction.'[47]

Encouraged by Fr Smyth, Mother Cecilia agreed to give him six sisters. A contract was drawn up and accepted, whereby the bishop undertook to guarantee the financial and temporal well-being of the sisters as well as their freedom to observe the Rule of their Institute without interference. Before their departure Mother Cecilia appointed Sister Ursula Frayne as Superior of the group, and before they left England the bishop confirmed her as 'Mother Superior of the Convent of Mercy, Australia.'

Sister Ursula Frayne 1817–1885

Clara Frayne was born in Dublin in 1817 and entered Baggot Street Convent in July 1834, three years after the foundation of the Institute by Catherine McAuley. On her profession day she took the name Ursula. Of the five other sisters and one postulant who had been assigned to the Australian mission, all but one were under the age of 30.

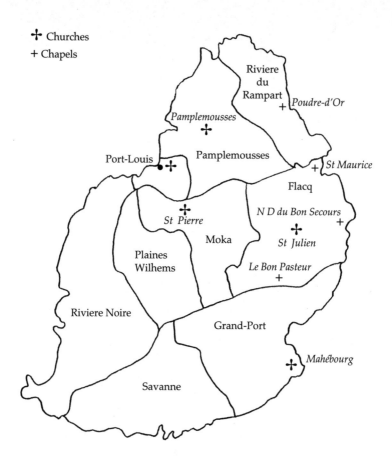

Mauritius
Districts and places of worship in 1841

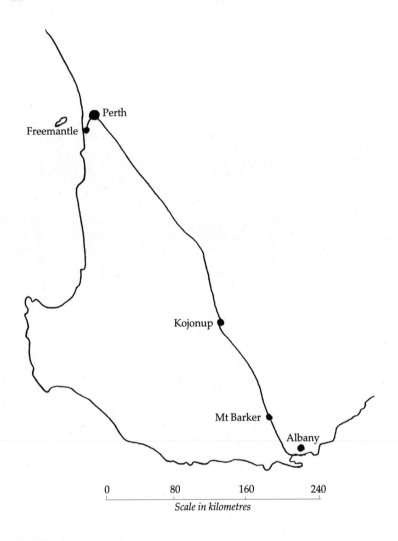

Perth

Freemantle

Kojonup

Mt Barker

Albany

| 0 | 80 | 160 | 240 |

Scale in kilometres

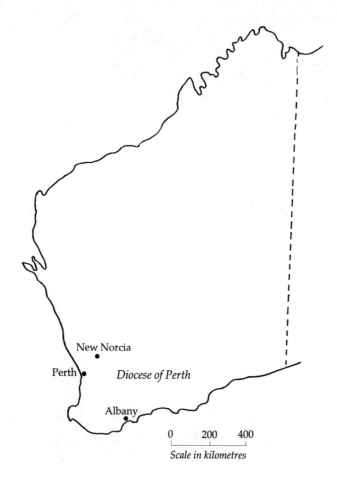

New Norcia

Perth

Diocese of Perth

Albany

0   200   400

Scale in kilometres

Western Australia

A portrait of Fr Libermann, reconstructed from an1845 image.

P. Thévaux

P. Thiersé

Bishop John Brady

Sr Ursula Frayne

Joseph Benedict Serra

Rosendo Salvado

Fr Noel Fitzsimons,
discoverer of the site of Santa Maria Mission,
Lake Mollyalup, near Mt Barker, 150 km from Albany.

PART II

Outward Bound

On 17 September 1845, the *Elizabeth* sailed from the port of Gravesend south of London with Bishop Brady and 27 missionaries. Among them were seven priests: the two Spanish Benedictines – Serra and Salvado; Dom Confalonieri, a Benedictine from the Italian Tyrol; an Irish diocesan priest, Father Peter Powell; and the three French priests of the Holy Heart of Mary Society – Thévaux, Bouchet, and Thiersé. The party also included an English Benedictine sub-deacon, Denis Tootle, and a French Benedictine novice, Léandre Fonteinne; the two brothers of the Holy Heart of Mary, Théodore Odon and Vincent Eusèbe; Signor Nicolas Caporelli, lay teacher, and eight Irish 'student catechists': John O'Reilly, Nicholas Hogan, John Gorman, Timothy Donovan, John Fagan, William Fowler, Martin Butler, and Terence Farrelly. Finally, there were six Irish Sisters of Mercy: Mother Ursula Frayne (Superior), Sr Catherine Gogarty (Assistant Superior), Sr Anne Xavier Dillon, Sr Mary Baptist O'Donnell, Sr Mary Ignatia de la Hoyde, Sr Mary Aloysius Kelly, and Catherine O'Reilly, Postulant.

The sisters were hoisted on board in a device like a wine cask cut in half. It was called a 'whip,' really a herring barrel minus its cover with a temporary seat inside. Sister Anne Xavier was the first to be packed inside the barrel, but as she was being hauled into the air the seat collapsed and she was found at the bottom of the barrel, to the great amusement of her fellow sisters.

In her letters home to Dublin Mother Ursula gave a detailed description of the ship she called 'our floating home':

Viewed from the shore it looked like a fine large three-masted ship with three decks – upper, intermediate and lower; this last was called the hold, where most of the merchandise, objects, etc. not wanted were stowed away. The intermediate deck had cabins and accommodation for passengers of the second class. The upper deck merits a more particular description. It was, or seemed to us, about 155 feet in length and was apparently divided into three equal parts – of which that in the centre was called 'midship' and was taken up with skylights and other contrivances for conveying light and air to the lower decks. At the end of the vessel was our refectory and our cells, or in the ordinary sea parlance, the saloon and cabins for the first-class passengers. Of the other end I had no near view – it was called the forecastle, and was occupied principally by the sailors. By an easy ascent of some dozen steps one arrived at what might be called the roof of the saloon. The proper name was 'poop'. A stout handrail all round prevented any danger of falling into the sea, and hen coops at each side made very good seats.[48]

Travelling first-class did not bring comfort. Ursula relates that their sleeping quarters…

…dignified by the name of 'cabins,' were about six feet by four feet with two shelves, one above the other, serving as bunks. Between the bunks and the wall there was barely standing room for one person, and how we managed to live in them for four months without injury to health is marvellous. There were not enough cabins for all, and five of the missionaries had to sleep without bunks or mattresses on the bare planks.

Shortly before the ship hoisted sail, Bishop Brady assembled his flock on deck and in a few words prepared them for the perils of the voyage ahead. They had scarcely entered the English Channel when they ran into mountainous seas. Dom Salvado ventured out of his cabin to have a look and was thrown flat on his face. He managed to creep back to his cabin, where he collapsed, sore in every bone, with a ferocious headache and vio-

lently seasick. Still ahead lay a voyage of almost four months.
Léandre Fonteinne reported in his letters:

> All that night and all the following day there was constant
> weighing and casting of the anchor. It was on the morrow
> that seasickness got a grip on everyone, with the exception of
> His Lordship and one of the catechists from Amiens. On the
> 18th, the wind blew very violently all day, though we had
> not yet even left the mouth of the Thames...Never would I
> have imagined that the English Channel could be so rough;
> for almost twelve whole days we were exposed to its
> caprices.[49]

October 3rd found them off the Madeira Islands; the sea had
calmed and life on board was organised. The Irish Sisters wryly
named the ship 'The Convent of Divine Providence,' and there
being no other saloon passengers, a certain order was assumed.
They rose at 4 am for a series of Masses, and each evening
Divine Office was chanted on deck. A letter from Mother Ursula
to Mother Cecilia gives details of the daily routine:

> At five in the evening, the Bishop in rochet [embroidered
> cloak], and stole, the priests in soutane, surplice and stole,
> two Benedictines who are also priests, in their religious
> habits, with large scapulars and cowls drawn over their
> heads, and all the students in secular clothes, sing vespers on
> deck. Your children sit at a distance; all other passengers and
> the sailors assemble at the end of the vessel and look on in ev-
> ident admiration and in profound silence; no sound is heard
> except that of rushing water; even the captain and officers
> gave orders to the seamen in whispers or by signs.

> The litany of Our Lady was sung at nightfall. This was some-
> thing of an occasion, as the Spanish Benedictine, Dom
> Salvado, had a magnificent voice and was also a first-rate
> musician. The remainder of the long days was passed by the
> men in giving and taking lessons in English and by the nuns
> reading, sewing and chatting.[50]

At times the elements caused upsets:

> Our good ship *Elizabeth* sometimes treats us unceremoniously;

fancy to yourself, a grave Sister of Mercy walking in slow religious pace across the cabin, when suddenly a lurch of the vessel prostrates her on the floor and rolls her from side to side; fortunately the room is not very large or her poor bones might be broken. You would be delighted to see us all well and happy.[51]

The presence of uncloistered nuns – the Sisters of Mercy being a relatively recent Order – was a new experience for the priests and seminarians used to nuns staying behind closed doors. Many grumbled at Bishop Brady. Léandre Fonteinne wrote: 'He is bringing out 27 people, eight of whom are of no use to him. The Tyrolese [Angelo Confalonieri] considered the expense of bringing these women an utter waste, especially with regard to the seventh member of the group who is not a religious at all but seems to be following His Lordship out in order to be his housekeeper... These women religious are entirely useless, and are more so in as much as His Lordship lets himself be influenced by them.'[52]

Obviously, the women were watched closely. No wonder Sister Catherine Gogarty remarked, 'A ship reminds me of a country town where people have little to do but watch their neibours [sic] and remark on their conduct.'

As for Bishop Brady and the Irish catechists, Fonteinne wrote:
The whole time, Dom Serra and Dom Salvado keep saying : 'Oh, if only our Bishop had the heart of the Abbot of Solesmes he'd be treating us as his sons and not as paid hands.' Suffice it to say it's a terrible thing to be born Irish. In truth, ever since I began to live with people of that nation, I've been convinced that to be born such is a punishment from on high. To love such people, you need to consider them as back on their own island, with the wide ocean right between them and you.[53]

But of his fellow Frenchmen Fonteinne had a more favourable opinion:
These Amiens priests are good, devout men but I feel they

keep too much to themselves. Doubtless that stems from their youth, but even more so from their having been educated by the Sulpicians. Their way of doing things is the right way, their plan of action the best possible. That's the sum of how they think-almost a table of contents of all their thinking. They are certainly gifted, but no one has managed to teach them to make effective use of it. I do believe they will do good on the mission.[54]

The priests of the Holy Heart of Mary had their own community regulation. At their first port of call at Capetown, Thévaux sent a letter to Libermann with the details:

4 am	Rising
4.30	Morning Prayer
5.30	Mass
6.15	Scripture Reading
7.00	English Language Study
8.30	Breakfast
9.00	Recreation
10.00	Office - Little Hours
11.15	Rest, study of theology and English
11.45	Particular Examination of Conscience
12.00	Recreation
12.30	Vespers
1.30	Spiritual Reading in French
2.30	Visit to the Blessed Sacrament
2.50	Study
3.00	Dinner
3.30	Recreation
4.30	Spiritual Reading in English, with all the missionaries
5.00	Divine Office, Study
6.30	Tea, and for me Religion Class for the Brothers
7.00	Recreation
8.15	Rosary, Night Prayer
9.00	Bedtime[55]

Father Thiersé made the wry remark that the daily regimen made him feel he was back in the ascetic ethos of the noviciate!

Happy though they were, the harsh reality of life brought much suffering. All were very seasick. Father Thiersé, after an extreme fit of vomiting one morning, had only one wish: to die! Father Bouchet replied, prophetically, 'Don't rejoice too much at seeing God soon, for it is His will that you'll live longer than any of us.' That turned out to be true, for Thiersé survived until 1880. Bouchet went on to say, 'It is you who will suffer and work the most in the new mission. In six months, I'll be no more, and three other confrères will soon follow me. You, you will remain a certain time alone amongst the natives to work for the salvation of those poor souls.' Father Thiersé often revisited this strange prophecy, which is documented in a letter to his mother.[56]

After recovering from his seasickness, Father Thiersé developed an inflammation of the feet that prevented him from standing. This resulted from the bizarre circumstances that the party had no change of shirts or stockings – they were wearing the same clothes in which they had left France! As they reached the tropics, conditions became intolerable. Thiersé wrote, '…the lice were devouring our backs.' There was in fact linen aboard, but it had been stored below decks with the baggage in the ship's hold. The captain of the *Elizabeth* refused to open the hold while they were at sea, insisting they must wait until they reached the Cape.

Having Brady's assurance in London that all necessities would be provided, Thévaux had requested fresh linen shortly after the voyage began. He was put off, and when by the end of October nothing had been done, Thévaux demanded an explanation. Only then did Brady admit that the shirts could not be got out, and offered four of his own. In a letter to Libermann from the Cape on October 22, Thévaux wrote: 'His Lordship was so good to give us the shirts that he was reduced to the same situation as ourselves. He was obliged to wash his own. He gave bed sheets to the sisters to make shirts. We are very grateful to him.'

Many years later, in answer to accusations against him by Bishop Salvado, Brady responded by blaming Thévaux:

I had fully warned the missionaries to bring a case with all they would need on the voyage, but unfortunately the young superior of that Congregation, believing that another was directing his confrères, neglected my advice and so the poor missionaries suffered the distress ... the young superior was a headstrong man (like the Benedictines), full of himself and little disposed to take advice. I was obliged to give them shirts, etc., and the Mercy Sisters worked constantly to provide them with shirts throughout the voyage.[57]

Stopover at Capetown

The good ship *Elizabeth* finally dropped anchor in Capetown Bay on 23 November. Mother Ursula described their arrival in a letter to Rev Mother di Pazzi at Baggot St Convent, Dublin:

Capetown is built at the foot of a hill called Table Mountain from its flat appearance, and being covered every morning by a tablecloth of snow-white clouds which the sun quickly removes. At first sight it seemed rather uninviting, but on a nearer approach we saw several nice houses all with flat roofs, well-cultivated gardens and cornfields in abundance ... but to return to my story:

The sailors are all standing waiting for orders to furl sails, which orders are at last given, and in two minutes the ship which was in full dress had not, in nautical phrase, a single stitch of canvas out, the anchor is dropped and we are assailed on all sides by boats from the shore, rowed by Africans, containing oranges and other fruits peculiar to the climate, bread, pipes, soap, etc. etc. In one boat there was a Caffre and some Hottentots; they were dressed like European sailors with the exception of one whose hat was exactly like a parasol made of reeds, with a hole in the centre to admit his head. They all wore great silver rings larger than ours on the little finger... You can hardly imagine with what pleasure we viewed land this evening, even though it is not that of our adoption. No one who has not made a voyage of nearly three months could know what a relief the sight of even a barren rock would be to eyes accustomed to look at nothing but sea and sky, or by way of variety at the sails and rigging. If any of our Darling Sisters are going on a voyage of the kind again, let them bring plenty of apples, oranges, jam and gingerbread.[58]

The Captain planned a short stay in port. Leaving the nuns on board, the missionaries went ashore and met the Vicar Apostolic, Dr Griffith, OP, who had only six to eight priests to cover his vast territory. Libermann's sons immediately thought this a good place to open a mission, since every ship on route to Bourbon [Réunion], Australia and the East made an obligatory landfall at the Cape.

By the first of December the Captain had finished his business. He had weighed anchor when a sudden squall pushed his ship into another anchored nearby, lodging *Elizabeth's* jib boom in the other ship's rigging. After a few days' delay for repairs, the voyagers departed on 3 December 1845.

Father Thévaux, in a postscript to a letter sent to Libermann from the Cape, said he failed to get any inkling from Bishop Brady as to where he or the others were to be posted on arrival: 'Every attempt I made he evaded by turning the conversation. We finally found our linen in the half-hold.'[59]

Father Maurice Bouchet falls ill

It looked like plain sailing as they headed east for Fremantle, Western Australia. Alas, for the missionaries of the Holy Heart of Mary, their calvary was only beginning. It appears that Fr Bouchet got sunstroke from going about bareheaded. On the morning of their departure they were able to say Mass at the Cape, after which Bouchet gave Father Thiersé to understand that he feared it would be his (Bouchet's) last.

A few days out of port Bouchet became mentally ill. He cried out that he was damned to hell's fire, a heretic who had composed a prayer to St Joseph addressing him as the real father of our Lord. At times he became very violent:

He tried several times to throw himself into the sea and to

strangle himself; we had to watch him night and day: several
times he nearly killed us when we approached him. For several days he uttered terrible cries saying he was already suffering hell's fire. Later on he made out that he was tricked
into becoming a priest, duped by Father Superior, a Jew. The
Congregation was an assembly of hypocrites with a false air
of modesty and piosity when in reality they were full with
ambition.[60]

Thévaux wrote: 'We could hardly hold him down on the bed;
we were forced to tie him down, putting on handcuffs and a sort
of straightjacket. This continued for the first fifteen days without
a break.' In this same letter Thévaux continued:

These events naturally attracted the curious to visit Bouchet,
and he often satisfied their curiosity with outbreaks of vio-
lence. He railed against the English: 'Oh, those English ras-
cals! Oh, that cursed race. Lord, deliver me from the English,
better leave me in hell'... Later, he examined the conscience
of a priest or two who came to amuse themselves at what he
said. They didn't return! To the sisters who came he yelled:
'Get out, you will give me bad thoughts. Get out! Oh, what
impurity!' Even mocking Bishop Brady, he said 'Ah, how
miserable I am, what a hell I merit. I am a cheat, a double
dealer... I have tricked priests and made them miserable, I
have fooled bishops, archbishops, cardinals, and Our Holy
Father, the Pope. I am a hypocrite all round. Ah, wretched
that I am. I've lost the whole mission ... poor priests assassinated ... sisters lost. Ah, cursed as I am, I have become a
heretic, I am placed at the head of a schism, I am suspended, I
am excommunicated!!!' The Bishop blanched and never
came again. He realised that although Bouchet was speaking
in the first person, despite his madness he was not duped: he
saw clearly into the future...[61]

Bouchet's illness must have been very hurtful and humiliating
to Thévaux and Thiersé, especially in front of the passengers.
'Our sick man, in his madness, seemed to be possessed. He tore
off his blue scapular, threw away his medal, rosary beads and

crucifix … he did not want to know anything about God, the sacraments, Our Lady. For 34 days he pronounced no other words except: *desiderium peccatorum peribit*, I am cursed, I am damned.'[62] Thévaux was convinced he had lost his mind.

Arrival at Fremantle

At last, on 7 January 1846 land was sighted, and next day they cast anchor at Fremantle. Mother Ursula recorded that two large boats took them to the landing place a mile away…

> En route the priests chanted the litany of the saints and other sacred canticles. When we landed, the *Te Deum* was intoned and the Bishop gave his solemn Episcopal blessing, the first ever witnessed in this country. All the European inhabitants were assembled on the shore attracted by curiosity. We saw two of the natives. They are a dark copper colour, their hair long, hanging in ringlets on their shoulders, their teeth of dazzling whiteness. They are perfectly erect, very tall and of most majestic appearance, as if they felt they were the lords of the soil. In general they wear a sort of cloak of kangaroo skin fastened on the right shoulder and under the left arm. They seem to be remarkably intelligent. We taught one little girl to make the sign of the Cross in about five minutes. Perhaps I should not call her girl, as although scarcely twelve years old, she was the mother of three children.[63]

All this time Père Bouchet sat disconsolately in an armchair, surrounded by some of the Irish students in case he should suffer another embarrassing outbreak.[64] A doctor was called, and Bouchet was declared to be in serious danger; that night Thévaux gave him the last sacraments.

Perth

On the next day, the 9th of January, they set sail for Perth, about 12 miles up the Swan River. Dom Salvado described the scenery:

> The majestic eucalyptus trees, the thick green shrubbery, bushes partly burned, sights of river banks covered with verdure … forming a contrast so varied and so brilliant that each tortuous curve of the Swan offered us every moment a new

scene, a new occasion to praise the Lord. Sometimes the sandy soil projected out almost to the middle of the river. There we observed numerous water birds, mostly pelicans, which ignored our approach. As for the swans, after which the river gets its name, there were none in sight.[65]

After a pleasant three-and-a-half-hour journey, Perth came into view. Again they sang: the Litany of Our Lady, the Ave Maris Stella, the Benedictus. A great crowd met them and followed them in procession to the little church, the first stone of which had been laid by Bishop Brady on his first visit to Perth. It was a simple structure – just four walls and a shingle roof, with no doors, windows or altar.

As they came out of the little church in the afterglow of the sunset, Bishop Brady informed the nuns that no prior arrangements had been made for their accommodation. Their arrival was totally unexpected. Ursula replied, 'We stood in the wilds of Australia on that midsummer night, and we could truly say with our Divine Model, "We have nowhere to rest our heads."'[66]

Undaunted, they went back the way they had come and eventually found an inn (by Perth standards) owned by a Mrs Crisp, a Methodist who was more than astonished at meeting nuns for the first time in her life. They found her kind and motherly.

Next day it was down to work to prepare the church for a solemn High Mass the following day, Sunday. Writing to her friends in Dublin, Mother Ursula described the building:

> The church – what was it like? Imagine a room about 30 feet long by 15 wide and 12 feet high; a shingle roof, through which the sun moon and stars could be distinctly seen; a few planks laid loosely on the ground did duty as flooring; no doors, no windows; an old wooden counter, the gift of a retired shopkeeper, served for altar. A faded green tablecloth, with yellow corners, did duty as an antependium, and a strip of calico, unhemmed, was the only altar-cloth. Such was the church and its furniture; yet poor as it was, it bore testimony

to the undying faith of the Irish Catholics, for it was the offering of a few Catholics. Some gave their time, others gave materials, while a few gave their mite in cash.[67]

A very handsome Tabernacle, crucifix and candlesticks which the Bishop brought with him; really beautiful vestments from Lyons; monstrance, chalice and other sacred vessels very good. Altogether when the altar was lighted up and the congregation assembled, the Church presented a sight not easily forgotten.

Next day the church was full to capacity, with the few Catholics and many Protestants drawn by the Solemn High Mass celebrated by Bishop Brady. Father Salvado played the piano (brought by the Mercy Sisters from London) and sang magnificently.[68]

Death of Father Bouchet

There were three Protestant Churches in Perth, and the arrival of such a host of Catholics caused some consternation among them. The Rev John Smithies, a Methodist missionary, wrote to his Head Office in London, 26 September 1846: 'The arrival of such a host was unexpected even to the Romanists here, and was an attempt to proselytise us by storm.'[69]

The party's reception in Perth was further aggravated by the erratic behaviour of the ailing Father Bouchet. Contrary to the diagnosis they had received in Fremantle, a more optimistic physician in Perth declared that the priest was in no danger of death and could be cured! Hardly had they settled in when 'Bouchet again made an attempt to destroy himself. He roared so loudly, that the neighbours rushed in thinking he was being assassinated.'[70]

Thiersé suggested that they treat his condition just as the insane were being handled in Europe at that time – by pouring water on his head and rapping his fingertips with a cane. Thévaux wrote, 'The treatment had its effect, but it cost us dearly. He cried out that he was being assassinated.'

The neighbours were scandalised, and even the local physician reproached Thiersé: '…you do not treat a priest like that … his insanity is the product of your bad treatment.' During the doctor's visits, it seems that Bouchet was relatively calm, but at other times he was uncontrollable. One day he dove through a closed window, bloodying his face, and fled into the woods; Thiersé chased him, and poor Bouchet was brought back to the house by force. This event proved to be the last straw. The Governor ordered Bouchet to be committed, and, thanks to the intervention of Bishop Brady – despite the public outcry to hang Thiersé – judicial proceedings were avoided.

By 23 January Bouchet's condition had deteriorated considerably. On the following morning he awoke remarkably lucid, repeating over and over '…Laetatus sum in his quae dicta sunt mihi: in donum domini ibimus…' (I am glad when I hear them say to me, let us go to the house of the Lord. Psalm 122). There was no trace of his former despair, and he showed a resolute confidence and desire to go to heaven. At 11 am he died, at the age of 25, a holy and edifying death, with the final words, 'Our (or Your) house will last: but it will only be by the Cross; I see the Cross… I see the Cross.' Thus did Father Maurice become the first priest to die in Western Australia. Thévaux reported to Libermann that

> He died as a saint. Those who had helped us to serve him loved him very much, but when he was dead they all agreed that he was in heaven. The doctor shed tears and asked to take part at his funeral. As for us, dear father, we do not know, neither Father Thiersé nor I, what sentiments prevailed on us. I could not rejoice for having lost our greatest support of the mission, and I could not be sad for my confrère to have gone to heaven, and so I have a mixed feeling of sadness and joy even to this day.
>
> After the death of our confrère we rendered him the last service of burial. Father Thiersé and I washed his body and dressed him with the habit and priestly vestments. He was exposed in state for three days, and in spite of the excessively hot weather, not only did no unpleasant odour come from

his body but his countenance appeared brighter than when alive, and the room where he was kept was all that time full of people.[71]

Two days later, after Office and solemn High Mass sung by Father Thévaux, Father Bouchet was buried behind the church by special permission of the Governor – a privilege not even accorded to Protestants.[72]

The Sisters found a suitable house on St George's Terrace, which Bishop Brady blessed on 17 January as their new home, the 'Convent of the Holy Cross.' They moved in without tables, beds, or mattresses, and only a few chairs, one sofa, and the piano. Nevertheless they were pleased with their surroundings: 'The town is like a beautiful garden, the trees are always green and covered with leaves … figs, vines, olives and melons grow spontaneously.'[73]

As for the town of Perth itself, Dom Salvado described it as follows:

There was very little of interest in the buildings or their layout. One could say that the town was half-bush, for a lot of the original trees were still there in streets and squares and by the houses, many of which are shaded from the sun by thick-leafed eucalyptus. We found the mosquitoes very troublesome, and the croaking of the frogs in marshy, stagnant waters here and there within the town limits was so loud that at times we sometimes had to raise our voices as if talking to the deaf.[74]

Dispersal of the Missionaries

From this point the missionaries were anxious to be on their way. To the French Fathers of the Holy Heart of Mary, Bishop Brady proposed the Vicariate of King George Sound, allowing the men to believe they had a choice. He so touted the advantages of the place that they readily accepted.

The Sound had a healthier climate, with less extreme heat in the summer, while the Vicariate of Port Essington (close to the modern city of Darwin) was quite remote (3,000 miles from

Perth), and so hot that the forests occasionally caught fire.
Moreover, Albany – the port in King George Sound – was a regular port of call for international shipping, while Port Essington
was practically cut off from the outside world. More insidiously,
there was another reason for Brady's manoeuvre: he wished to
reserve the wilds of Port Essington for Confalonieri, to prevent
his knowledge of what was going on in Perth, and to limit the
Italian's ability to send adverse reports back to his friend in
Rome, the Rector of the Propaganda College.[75]

To reach Port Essington in those days, one had to sail by way
of Sydney.

Confalonieri departed Perth on March 1st with two Irish catechists, James Fagan and Nicholas Hogan. For their sole support, Bishop Brady had provided only two cases of books which
they might sell when they reached Sydney, and so they were
forced to borrow money in order to continue their voyage from
that city.

They departed Sydney on 6 April on board the schooner
Heroine. In the Endeavor Straits they were shipwrecked, and the
two catechists drowned, along with all hands except the captain
and Father Confalonieri, who were rescued by a Newfoundland
dog named 'Nelson.' They were eventually picked up by the
Enchantress and the priest made his way to Port Essington.

The Protestant Commandant, John McArthur, helped
Confalonieri set up his mission at Smith's Point, near present-
day Darwin. He found seven native tribes in his area, and drew
an accurate map of the territory which still survives. He also
compiled a vocabulary of the dialects, and wrote a short prayer
book in the Iwaija dialect of the natives of Port Essington. On 9
June 1848 he died during an influenza epidemic, leaving a community of some 400 Christians behind him. The Commandant
wrote to Archbishop Polding in Sydney, '...his remains were accompanied to the tomb by the officers and military with all the
respect that was due to a man so highly esteemed.'[76]

Confalonieri had received a substantial sum of money from
the Propaganda office in Ireland but he was completely ignored

by Bishop Brady. In February 1846 (before leaving for Perth) he had written to his friend, the Rector of Propaganda in Rome, seeking financial aid for his mission. He asked that the money be sent by way of Sydney… '…for I am certain, after bitter experience, that if that help reaches the hands of Bishop Brady first, he will direct it to his own mission and I would get absolutely nothing, even though I would be happy to receive only 300 [francs].'[77]

The French fathers had already formed their own opinion of the bishop. At the end of January 1846, Thévaux wrote to Father Libermann: '…the Bishop treats us as children; it seems to me that if he could send us away with nothing, he would do so. He uses all his shrewdness and deviousness to achieve his plans. He has already alienated all his priests, who only long for the day when they can leave.'[78]

In the same letter, Thévaux announced good news: one of the young Irish students, Timothy Donovan, asked to join the Congregation. The bishop had intended to found a seminary and a college, but finding that impossible, he allowed the students to join the missionaries. Thévaux joyfully accepted him: 'He is very pious and was exemplary on the journey out. He had already, in Dublin, studied with the Franciscans and helped them in their apostolic works. Undoubtedly, God had chosen him to replace Père Bouchet. Since he speaks English, he could be of great help to us; if some day he has to return to Europe he could be of great service as a teacher of English in the noviciate. We ourselves will teach him theology and send him to Perth for his ordination.'[79]

Thévaux also spoke enthusiastically of the natives: 'They love us … they are with us every day; we live in an isolated house in the woods, and our poor natives are in our yard from morning to night. When they come in the morning, you can hear them half a mile away – shouting, laughing, joking, like children at play … they are as simple as two-year-old children in our country: they do not think of anything, they do not possess anything; they want nothing but to live without a care or worry.'

That would seem to indicate that for the moment the only reason they attached themselves to the missionaries was the bits of food they got... 'The king himself came with his wife... The Royals did not disdain to accept a small piece of bread that we offered them and considered themselves obliged to gobble it down straightaway; then they sat down on the sand right beside the kitchen, which was the strategic position par excellence.'[80]

While waiting to leave for Albany, the Holy Heart of Mary missionaries made a five-day retreat and Brother Vincent made his apostolic consecration. Father Thévaux ends his letter with a list of the things 'His Lordship' judged appropriate for their mission: '...45 shirts, 22 handkerchiefs, 4 towels, 7 pairs of long stockings, 20 bed sheets...' [with 45 shirts they were indeed well provided for, but 4 towels and 7 pairs of stockings!] '...For the chapel we received two chalices, one set of vestments, one set of cruets, two flasks for the holy oils and lastly an incense thurible.'[81]

The Benedictines

The Benedictines were assigned a central mission northeast of Perth. Their party consisted of two priests, Frs Joseph Benedict Serra and Rosendo Salvado; the French novice, Léandre Fonteinne, of the Abbey of Solesmes; and the Irish catechist John Gorman. The other Benedictine, Denis Tootle, stayed in Perth because of bad health.

Before departing they met a generous Irishman, one Captain Scully, who was a relation of Mother di Pazzi of the Mercy Convent in Dublin. He was the chief magistrate of an inland settlement near Bolgart Springs, about seventy miles north of Perth. He offered to transport their goods free of charge, and provided two drays to carry their provisions, which included tools, farm implements and a portable altar. By nightfall on 21 February they reached Bolgart Springs, and the next morning they moved further to a remote locality called Noona-Gonda.

In a counter-memorandum written in 1850-51, Bishop Brady claimed that due to lack of sufficient resources he wished to keep the remaining missionaries in Perth until additional money arrived, the 55,000 francs he had received from the Society of the Propagation of the Faith having been spent on the voyage out and on necessary expenses. He saw this as an opportunity for them to learn English as well as the native language, '...but the Benedictines and the stubborn young superior of the Congregation of the Holy Heart of Mary insisted on going, and unfortunately I submitted. I gave them the portion I could not refuse ... that and my blessing.'[82]

It seems likely that the bishop was not upset to see them go. If he was as bereft of resources as he claimed, how did he plan to provide for the missionaries in the long months ahead? Pursuing his favourite projects – in addition to supporting the sisters and completing the little chapel – had put him deep in debt. And later on he would repeatedly be accused of diverting funds from the Society of the Propagation of the Faith (which were intended for the missionaries) to profit the whites in Perth.

While it is clear that money played a prominent role in Bishop Brady's life, there is no evidence that he used it for his own personal gain; he was simply a hopeless administrator. To get out of difficulties he went into debt, and as debts accumulated he was forced to borrow even more.

Bishop Brady's Private Life

Privately, Bishop Brady led a rather austere life, eating the poorest of food and living in a succession of makeshift rooms. A letter from Mother Ursula describes him living in the church belfry:

> His third habitation was the belfry! A little wooden building, just like those boxes that you may have seen at a sea bathing place except that the boards of which it was made are much fewer and farther between, in fact there is free access to the weather on all sides; here the Bishop lived both day and night, until the rainy season compelled him to seek shelter in another little room near the church, where he has barely space to stand beside a sofa on which he endeavours to take some rest.[83]

Dr Madden, sent out as Secretary to the Colony at Perth, paid this tribute to the bishop: '... in the performance of his clerical duties, I mean, administering the Sacraments, assisting at the altar, visiting the sick, promoting the education of the poor ... in assisting the distressed, and above all in dealing charitably and kindly with the poor natives, I can safely say that the conduct of Dr Brady was most exemplary. He lived in a miserable hovel without comforts of any kind, on the simplest food; his diet was to my certain knowledge coarse and poor, but often scanty in the extreme.'[84]

Bishop Brady was to find great support in Dr Madden, primarily in resisting the partisan bias of the Legislative Assembly in Swan River:

On my arrival in the Swan River settlement, of which I was Colonial Secretary, I found Dr Brady contending single-handed against the entire local Government, every member of which, with two exceptions, was bitterly opposed to Catholicity. The colony was administered by Irish Orangemen for the interests of Orangeism. Lord Grey (Secretary of State for the Colonies) knew this, and being determined to break down that Government of a faction, sent out a Roman Catholic as Secretary, the first Catholic ever appointed – myself. I found Dr Brady battling for his mission stoutly and sincerely, not always discreetly or effectually, with a set of unprincipled astute bigots in authority. But he established the mission, and he maintained it in spite of them up to the time of my arrival. Without his pertinacity, and I would say daring, in confronting powerful opposition, in contending against adverse circumstances of the most formidable kind, the mission never could have been established. From the time of my arrival I took care that Dr Brady and his mission were no more troubled, disturbed, or warred with.[85]

Libermann's Men Depart
for The Sound

The French party for King George Sound left from Perth on 8 February 1846; it consisted of Frs Thévaux and Thiersé and the two lay Brothers, Vincent and Théodore. With them the bishop sent Father Peter Powell and the clerical student, Timothy Donovan, a possible candidate for the Congregation of the Holy Heart of Mary.

Powell was the only experienced man among them. Ordained in 1842, he had worked in several parishes in England and Ireland. He was enlisted now merely to lead the party to Albany and then to return to take up duties at Guildford, east of Perth. The journey to Albany, 313 miles away, was to take 18 days on foot through bush country. They could have gone more comfortably by ship but the bishop ruled this out as being too expensive. On the day they left, His Lordship asked Thévaux for a testimonial letter, acknowledging that they were going where he appointed them and that they were satisfied with the arrangements. In defence of this strange and unusual request he would ask a similar testimony from all the missionaries on their departure.

Just as they were leaving, Bishop Brady handed Thévaux his letter of faculties. Because it was too dark to read the letter right away, Thévaux had to wait until they reached their first halting site. In the light of the campfire he read: 'Rev Fr Superior, Very Rev Fr Joostens, now at the Sound, is my Vicar General and so for the moment I have to defer making new arrangements, so hereby, I give you all the faculties necessary to commence and continue the important mission to the natives of the Sound.'[86]

Thévaux immediately realised that the bishop was not going

to keep his agreement with Libermann to grant them their own vicariate, since he had confined their jurisdiction to the natives only. The very next morning he fired back a letter to the bishop:

> I requested him to explain the vague terms: 'all the faculties necessary'; I complained that I was not informed of the presence of a vicar general in the district and moreover, my faculties were reserved to one category (the natives). His Lordship had forgotten the principal clause in the agreement between us: that the Congregation alone would be in charge of the vicariate.

> With our powers limited to the natives, we would be unable to give spiritual help to the Europeans, not to mention to Frenchmen, should they require our aid. To stretch it to the limit, we could not hear the confessions of the community since we are not natives! Moreover, it could be added that since no natives were as yet baptised, the faculties had no objective.[87]

The letter, though firm in tone, was respectful. He wished to know the precise extent of the powers given to him, recalling the agreement made at La Neuville.

That same day a second disillusionment awaited Thévaux. On leaving Perth, the bishop placed Powell in charge of the party en route and while they organised their settlement at King George Sound. This was a measure of prudence, as their lack of knowledge of English did not make things any easier for them. In fact, however, Powell proceeded to take over as if he were the Superior of the group. In response to a challenge from Thévaux, Powell produced a letter from the bishop naming him superior of the group and envoy extraordinary to regulate the foundation at the Sound.

Thévaux: 'As a result, I told him that I accept him as my superior en route, arranging the halting sites and the times of meals. But as for our religious exercises *intra domum*, he better beware if he does not wish to have me resist him with a vigour he probably might not expect.'[88]

Thévaux then revealed all the engagements his Lordship had

accepted in La Neuville. Powell was absolutely astonished, since the bishop had given him to understand at the Cape of Good Hope that he (Powell) would take over the direction of the vicariate; he realised now that all the promises were only verbal and therefore of no value.

The physical aspect of their journey was equally unpleasant: there were no roads, it was the height of summer, and they were plagued by flies and mosquitoes and a shortage of water. On the evening of the first day of their trek through the bush, Thiersé sent a description of his new homeland to his mother back in Alsace:

I would like to give you a brief description of New Holland. This country is about seven or eight times the size of France, but it is quite uncivilised. There is none of the beauty of Europe here. No cultivation, only awesome forests on every side. There are many Jarrah and other trees which have beautiful flowers but no fruit. We have found only two kinds of edible root, but what is better is a kind of cane which tastes like chestnuts. I have been eating it these past few days, but somehow it does not seem to agree with me. Still, if we lack fruit, we have an abundance of meat. There is a kind of wild cat here called a kangaroo which is very plentiful: it is as large as a sheep. The woods are full of birds and the lakes full of swans and pelicans.

I would love you to see us having our meals; we have neither tables nor knives, nor forks, nor dishes, nor plates; our five fingers lend themselves to every task; the ground serves both as table and chairs and the vault of the sky forms our roof. You could not believe how much enjoyment we find under the beautiful sky; the sand is soft to sleep upon, and when there is no rain, a single blanket is sufficient to protect us from the chill of the dew. We have to keep a fire going all night to keep the snakes and scorpions away; the snakes, especially, are very dangerous: there is a very small one, the bite of which, they say, brings sudden and inevitable death to any man or animal it strikes. The savages say they are delicious to eat. You can see from that, that a missionary must not be fastidious. (My sister Françoise would not find it very congenial in these wild parts!) However, with the grace of God one can do anything.[89]

Later, in his report to Libermann, Thévaux wrote of Powell: 'He was 35-40 years old. He gave us plenty to suffer because of his quick temper and stubbornness during the whole of the 18-day trip... No one was exempt – Thiersé, the brothers – everyone was plagued incessantly. He forbade me one day to say Mass because I made an altar with mattresses on which I put the altar stone, having done this several times before and he himself had said Mass on such an altar.'[90]

Meanwhile, Bishop Brady sent Libermann Thévaux's testimonial of satisfaction, adding the following letter:

The Very Rev Father Joostens, my Vicar General and director of the Mission during my absence having settled at the Sound, I could not give Fr Thévaux the title and powers of Pro-Vicar at the Sound. The latter, in a letter just received, has complained in a rather unacceptable manner. I have just informed him that there were two reasons: the Government does not give foreigners land for the natives until they are British subjects for two years, and the Very Rev. Joostens, having settled at the Sound in my absence, and having formed a congregation there at Albion [Albany], I could not change the situation immediately, but in the meantime I have committed the care of the natives or aborigines to the fathers of the Holy Heart of Mary. I am happy to let you know the position. We need missionaries, but two principal qualities are necessary: good health and a little patience and good will.[91]

Arrival at Albany

Finally the party arrived at King George Sound, at the little port of Albany, sometimes called Albion or Alton. Powell, as Superior of the mission, rented a house for a year for the new arrivals. 'He also purchased some utensils for the kitchen, and some provisions for which I had to pay, so in the first few days at the Sound I already had spent more than half of the original £30 given to us by Bishop Brady,' Thévaux reported, and

At a solemn function on our arrival, the whole population of 100 – Catholic and Protestant – turned up. There were scarcely a dozen Catholics. They consisted of the Mooney family and a Dr Harrison. Everywhere Father Powell announced that the missionaries had come to look after the natives. He never once included the whole Vicariate.[92]

For Thévaux this clarified Bishop Brady's intentions:

It convinced me once more that he no longer wished to give us the complete mission but indeed to split it up. Father Joostens, however, is a good man about 70 years old; he is good and leaves us in peace. The Superior (supposedly!) of the Missionaries of the Holy Heart of Mary obtained faculties for us over the whites, until revoked... On Sunday Fr Joostens came to preach in our little chapel, which we built at the bottom of our garden. He speaks English more or less well. He wishes to leave soon. We will see then what His Lordship does to carry out our agreement.[93]

At the beginning of March, his mission accomplished, Powell returned to Perth carrying a letter from Thévaux to the bishop.

In the meantime, the missionaries didn't remain idle. They made contact with 30 or 40 natives who happened to be in the Sound at that time and tried to instruct them. They quickly found that the effectiveness of their mission was in direct proportion to the meals they provided. Instruction in Latin was given to the student Timothy Donovan for an hour each day, but he made slow progress. At the same time they explored the country round King George Sound, where, to their astonishment, they discovered no natives. The congregation for High Mass and Vespers on Sundays consisted of five or six Catholics and a few Protestants.

After Easter the missionaries explored further afield, up to 94 miles and beyond, looking for the aborigines.

I am now nearly certain [reported Thévaux] that there are
very few of them in the vicariate. At this present moment [1
June] there are not even 50 in the town, which is the one place
where you normally expect more. Further inland it is rare to
find any in the bush. If you wish to find them, it will be at the
farms and white settlements. Even there they are only a few. I
myself have gone as far as Kojonup 36 leagues or 113 miles
away. I visited two farms en route and found only a dozen,
some of whom I had already met in the Sound and had even
come to our catechism classes.[94]

On further expeditions of the same distance, they met normally
only 20 or so; one can imagine how frustrating this was to the
missionaries. They had to backpack food, including water, for
there was none in the bush – no fruit trees, no vegetables – and
on the way back they had to buy provisions at Protestant farms
at an exorbitant price.

'According to public rumour,' Thévaux continued, 'there
were more than 50,000 blacks in the King George Sound area. I
believed this at first, to my joy, but today [1 June] I reckon there
are not even 6,000 in the whole vicariate.'[95] Those figures were
far in excess of the real number: at the end of June, the
Lieutenant Governor assured them there were hardly 400 in all
the vicarate, and not more than 5,000 in Western Australia.
Where then were the reputed two million on the coast, not to
mention the interior?

Under these conditions the future looked bleak indeed. With
such a small population of aborigines dispersed over such a
wide area, with no fixed abode, what could be done? To attempt
to settle these nomads would be a utopian notion. They were
constantly on the move because the land was very unsuitable for
agriculture; to minister to them, the missionaries had no choice
but to follow them... but to where? An encampment of perhaps
10 aborigines might be here today and gone tomorrow, and they
usually travelled in groups of only three or four. To make matters worse, the missionaries had only a rudimentary knowledge
of English, and the natives were hardly more fluent. Their wan-

dering lives centred around food: it was a daily quest, and their best chance of obtaining food was near the farms.

'On our arrival at the Sound, the natives flocked to us when they learned we had come expressly for them, expecting abundance of food. We had nothing to offer except a little alms. We began catechising the children, which was followed by a simple meal. However, they soon left us because the Protestants gave them plenty of food.'[96]

Feeding the natives required money, and that soon ran out.

The Benedictines at Noona-Gonda

From the outset, Bishop Brady had placed the Benedictine missionaries well away from any inhabited area. For three months they followed the aborigines on their perpetual walkabouts, foraging for food and sharing their lizards, opossums and other delicacies. At the camp after the hunt, Salvado shrewdly observed their customs and in his notebook wrote down every new word.

They soon realised that Europeans could not lead that life indefinitely. If they wished to catechise the natives, they knew they would have to provide the necessities of life, and towards this end the missionaries had neither the money nor the supplies. In an effort to teach agriculture by example, the Benedictines set their sights on building a monastery which would become a centre for farming and cattle raising. They intended to purchase or rent land that would over the long term, it was hoped, tempt the aborigines to settle down.

Eventually this scheme would succeed, in the form of the still-surviving Abbey and town of New Norcia, but for now the missionaries were disheartened and half-starved. Salvado departed on foot for Perth to obtain funds for food and implements.

Back in Perth, the bishop appealed to the handful of local Catholics, but they had little to give. Then Salvado, who was a brilliant pianist (he had once charmed the royal family of Naples back at his monastery in Italy), hit on the idea of a recital. It was thought such an occasion might appeal to everyone, Catholic and Protestant alike. Even Governor Clark offered his assistance, and the event proved to be a resounding success. A generous Irish woman, noticing Salvado's broken boots, was moved to give him her own and walked home barefoot. With the proceeds from the concert, Salvado bought a pair of bullocks and some farm implements, and a local Protestant contributed a dray, with which the Spaniard then departed once again for his mission in the bush.

Brady's Reproach

Bishop Brady used the example of the Benedictines to goad Fathers Thévaux and Thiersé. In his letter of 3 April 1846 he demanded that they move out of Albany and establish themselves in the bush, well away from white settlements. A kind of trading post was to be set up a few miles from town where the aborigines could exchange goods with the Europeans. Just 11 days later, another letter from Brady reproached them for not moving to Kojonup, 113 miles north of Albany: 'The Benedictines followed my instructions to the letter and so were saved, even if the allocations from the Propagation of the Faith did not arrive; they had planted two acres of cleared land. Remember, God blesses the humble and the obedient.'[97]

This letter and the bishop's attitude were manifestly unjust: His Lordship was unaware of the group's explorations and privations since Father Powell had departed Perth a month earlier, and, in any case, Brady had never directed that the group establish themselves in the interior. (If he had, why would Powell have taken a year's lease on a house in Albany?) As for Kojonup, Thévaux had already been there and found it an under-provisioned military outpost manned by eight soldiers. Meanwhile, the community's funds were reduced to £2; they were living on vegetables from their house garden.

The friction between Brady and the Congregation in Albany wore on. His Lordship accused them of disobedience; Thévaux replied that he wished to obey, provided he was given the means to do so. Thévaux annoyed the bishop with his continual reminders of the agreement made at la Neuville: if His Lordship wished to divide the Mission, this order must come from Libermann.

At the beginning of June 1846, Joostens was recalled to Perth by the bishop and promised to plead their case for them. The rainy season had just begun, and for three months it would be impossible to venture into the bush. Thiersé and Thévaux were both ill, short of money, and ill equipped to relocate. Then, on 23 June the Vice-Governor informed them that the government had granted the Congregation the lands they had sought – *on one condition*: the farms were to be for the natives, under the control of the missionaries, but not to be sold to Europeans. If the missionaries should leave, the lands would revert to the Crown.

On 24 June Powell returned with the powers of Vicar General, bringing a rather conciliatory letter from Bishop Brady to the effect that he had always been disposed to give the vicariate to the Congregation, but they must wait two years until they had received British citizenship papers. For now they must be patient. In the meantime, Powell was charged to lead them into the interior to a mutually agreed outpost, where the missionaries would develop the land following the example of the Benedictines.

When Powell arrived back in Albany as the bishop's spokesman, the exchange was tense. Brady's suggestion that two outposts might be developed was out of the question, since it violated the rule of community life, and in any case, Thévaux had decided to send away Brother Théodore and the student Timothy Donavon. As Powell relayed the bishop's instructions, Thévaux countered that since the rainy season had already begun he could not reply directly but would be quite willing to do so afterwards, assuming the means were provided.

Thévaux's defence was sufficiently convincing for Powell to suddenly change his attitude and bare his soul. He spoke of the bishop and the debts that had accumulated for the upkeep of the sisters, the sad state of the mission, his fears for the future, and all that he had personally suffered at Brady's hands. Powell reasoned that for a town of 800 people, with only 100 Catholics and few natives, eight sisters and eight students were an unjustifiable expense. He advised the Congregation to obtain sole jurisdiction over the vicariate in order to secure direct funding from the Society of the Propagation of the Faith, and he recommended that Thévaux return to France to achieve this objective.

On his return to Perth, Father Powell revealed the dire poverty of the priests at the Sound. The bishop, learning that the missionaries had still not relocated, responded by suspending Powell for a period of 15 days. When Powell protested this censure and threatened to complain to Rome, the bishop relented. Heartsick on account of the beleaguered mission, Powell then demanded that he be allowed to travel abroad to raise funds. He soon departed for Batavia (Dutch East Indies) and Europe, never to return to Perth.

Ecclesiastical censure played a major role in Brady's administration. He suspended not only Powell, but also Thévaux and the Bendictines Salvado and Serra. For the laity who insisted that he pay his debts to them, his weapon was excommunication. In such an atmosphere, it is no wonder that Powell's departure was a source of concern and consternation for the bishop. On 13 September 1846 he wrote a pre-emptive letter to the Secretary of Propaganda:

> I've heard it said that some missionaries and others of no apostolic spirit have written or given false information on the number of natives, while these same people have made no effort to look for these poor people in the bush. It is true that we have no means to feed them in the interior. If Father Powell, an Irish priest, comes to Rome to complain, *nolite ascoltare eum, non est fide dignus* (do not listen to him, he is not worthy of credence).[98]

In June that year Brady had already complained of Thévaux to Libermann, claiming that he wished to honour the agreements that had been made, but that it was impossible because they were not English nationals. Now he reproached Thévaux directly in two letters:

I am informed by people worthy of belief, that you plan to seek the first opportunity to travel to Europe to complain of the way you have been treated. I wish to inform you that if you persist in leaving the mission confided to you I will withdraw all powers and faculties granted to you by me. [In such event, he went on to invite Thévaux to open a new mission closer to Perth, modelled on that of the Benedictines.] If you absolutely wish to go, then take your Congregation with you... If I could believe everything told me, you are in a position of being suspended from all ecclesiastical offices.[99]

We bought you tools to establish a base far from human habitation ... if you had been obedient, you would now have a flourishing mission instead of living in idleness and misery in Albany.[100]

On 15 September the Albany mission received their first letters from La Neuville, Amiens, but these had been written the preceding October, and they came not from Libermann himself but from Father Schwindenhammer. It would be another full year before Thiersé and Brother Vincent would hear any word. This lack of communication weighed heavily on them; they bore the responsibility of quitting Australia, without knowing Libermann's opinion, and they felt abandoned by the Congregation. Apparently Libermann *had* written to the colony, but for some reason these letters never arrived. A rumour current in Perth at the time – which must be treated with caution – held that the bishop burned all letters that passed through his hands.

Meanwhile, conditions in Albany had not improved. In a letter of 20 August 1846 Thiersé gave Libermann an account of their six months:

Up to the present I have done nothing. I have heard 11 confessions, baptised a child, administered four first communions (two were 30 years old). But if my ministry here does not amount to much, the fatigue and pain involved is not insignificant.

I made two treks into the woods... You can imagine the fatigue in covering 40 or 50 miles per day [doubtless he exaggerates]: all this with backpacking 30 pounds and a heavy shotgun. More fatigue in constructing a shelter and collecting timber to keep fires going all night, to prevent us perishing with the cold and also to keep at bay wild dogs and serpents. Then, soaked with sweat, we lie on the ground, abandoned to the hands of God, health and life.[101]

On 16 September Thévaux responded to two letters from His Lordship. Apparently Joostens, now cited by the bishop as a witness against the Congregation, played a double role. While at the Sound, Joostens had discouraged them from starting the mission or learning the language, or even making forays into the countryside. In response to the charge of spending money uselessly, Thévaux gave an exact accounting of the £30 they had received the previous February, adding that 'A local person gave me 10 shillings, which was a great help.'

Tales without reason

Thévaux was in the untenable position of defending himself against Joostens' charges while pleading for a rational appraisal of the mission in Albany. His letter to Brady of 16 September 1846 indicates that he was well aware of two facts that discredited the bishop: first, that Brady had failed to honour certain debts, resulting in the refusal of any credit whatsoever to the French missionaries; and second, that Brady had received a shipment of 40,000 pounds of flour from Adelaide, of which not one pound was sent on to those who needed it most. In light of these facts, Thévaux's calm humility is all the more noteworthy:

I consider myself obliged, My Lord, to make these revelations, so that Your Lordship might recognise his [Joostens'] deceit and not believe in future calumnies which the equability of a religious incurs almost daily on the part of secular Priests who are not able to tolerate this silent but eloquent lesson ... I ask and beg Your Lordship to believe that in my past conduct I have always tried to reconcile [Father Libermann's] orders with my other obligations. Your orders are sacred for me, My Lord, but the Congregation is my Mother and the small community which I have with me is dearer to me than my own life ... it surely does not astonish you that in the midst of so much which causes me grief and embarrassment that I have told you that I must first seek guidance in some of these affairs, so difficult and so delicate? But to tell tales without reason? No, My Lord, that does not please me, for these tales can never do good.[102]

PART III

The Final Straw

With Father Thiersé desperately ill, and all attempts to evacuate him having failed, the French missionaries' fortunes took an unexpected turn for the better at the end of the rainy season. The Captain of the French whaler *Le Cosmopolité* put into port at Albany and, witnessing the dire condition of his compatriots, donated 300 francs, flour, a bag of biscuits, and other provisions. Even this bit of luck encouraged them, and with the weather improving, Thévaux and Thiersé soon set out for Lake Mollyalup, about 40 miles north of Albany, and nine miles north of Mount Barker, to a mission site as proposed by Bishop Brady.

They took with them 15 days' supply of rice and bread, and tools to build a wooden house. For eight days they felled trees, but they returned to the Sound when their food ran out and they were exhausted by their unusual exertions. After eight days of rest, Thévaux went back to Mollyalup with Brother Vincent to continue the work, leaving Thiersé behind to look after their garden.

The Foundation of Santa Maria at Mollyalup

From this point forward, for the better part of the year, the priests made regular trips between the Sound and their new mission house. On 4 December 1846 Thévaux described the house in a letter to Brady:

> It consists of a Chapel, two small bedrooms, a kitchen, with an alcove for Brother Vincent off the kitchen; the kitchen also serves as our common room. We have been able to build with great difficulty a chimney from earth and wood, which taxed

all the art and industry of Father Thiersé, because we had no stones, and the soil would only hold its shape with great difficulty and would not keep together against the rain and the heat of the fire.[103]

On Christmas Day 1846 this new residence was named 'Santa Maria' and solemnly blessed. Today the site is marked by a commemorative tablet:

SANCTA MARIA
MOLLYALUP
THIS TABLET MARKS THE SITE AND HONOURS
FATHERS THÉVAUX AND THERESÉ WHO
ENDURED GREAT PRIVATIONS HERE ENDEAVOURING
TO ESTABLISH A MISSION FOR THE ABORIGINALS
IN THE YEARS 1846–47.
ERECTED BY THE PARISHONERS OF ALBANY AND
MOUNT BARKER 1976.[104]

The next week, Thévaux and Thiersé returned to the Sound to harvest their garden crops and make arrangements to move, in case the bishop should honour repeated pleas for money and provisions. But no word came, only continuing news of tumult and confusion in Perth. Brady had excommunicated two women, defamed others from the pulpit, and continued to pile up unpaid debts.

By the end of January 1847 Thévaux was left with only a few potatoes, and Thiersé and Brother Vincent, who were back at Santa Maria, survived by eating frogs. Presently, however, Thévaux was encouraged by a letter from Brady announcing that money had come from the Society of the Propagation of the Faith which would be shared with the mission at Albany.[105]

Anticipating this new infusion of support, Thévaux had high hopes. Thiersé, returning from Mollyalup and still in bad health, mocked him for his gullibility: 'We will get nothing from him unless, like the Benedictines, we force him.' The Benedictines had virtually blackmailed him by threatening to report him to Rome. By this means they had extracted six cart-loads of provisions from him at various times. Both men were aggravated by further news of rows with the Benedictines, Brady's refusal to honour his debts, and his farm of 10 cows and 500 sheep. And there was the rumour of the burnt letters. For men who believed they had been abandoned and who had to forage for food every day, such news must have left a bitter taste.

In a bittersweet letter of 10 February 1847 the bishop made it known that help was on the way, but its postscript was clearly threatening:

> Signor Caporelli has just told me things which strike me hard and so painful, since they come from you. Now I must tell you that if you have written all that I have been told, I will be obliged to suspend you and also report you to your Superior. I am also told that the French in Perth spread your scandalous letters about. You mix pious sentiments with all that. All disobedient priests act in the same way... Beware of false judgements, says Saint Paul. Remember, anyone who speaks ill or writes thus about a bishop is *ipso facto* suspended and excommunicated.[106]

We do not have Thévaux's letter to Caporelli in Perth, but it must indeed have been circulated. And since Caporelli was Consul for the Pontifical court, he let it be known that he was charged to report to Rome on the affairs in Perth, and the doings of Bishop Brady in particular.

Thévaux Confronts The Bishop

In response to Brady's threat, the Fathers at Albany decided they must give a personal account of their mission. On 28 February 1847 Thévaux set out for Perth, leaving behind Thiersé, who was still sick and seeking passage to Mauritius. Thévaux reached Perth on the evening of 14 March. He knew his interview with Brady would be painful but critical to the future of his mission. Moreover, without any instructions from Libermann, he would have full responsibility for that future. Going first to Caporelli for the latest news, he learned that tensions in the city had eased since Brady had paid his debts and seemed now to be on the defensive. This by no means meant that Thévaux's task would be easy, but the example of the Benedictines had shown that the bishop was most likely to be motivated by fear.

Meeting Brady at the church, Thévaux explained his financial situation and the medical conditions of Thiersé and Brother Vincent. His Lordship replied that they must all come to Perth, since they were clearly incapable of directing the mission at the Sound. Thévaux demurred, insisting that only Libermann had the authority to relieve them, and he challenged the bishop's allocation of resources among the various outposts. At this, His Lordship left, declaring that Thévaux was suspended from saying Mass. 'That is not the way to suspend,' countered the young French priest. 'My suspension will be lifted in Rome, and I will force you to give me money for my passage to Europe.'[107] So ended round one.

The next morning, Joostens informed Thévaux that the bishop had relented, that he *would* be allowed to say Mass, and that a second interview had been scheduled for that evening. This meeting included Joostens and Caporelli, and finally Thévaux got a hearing. He reproached the bishop for abandoning the mission at Albany and announced his intention to return to Europe with his confréres to report to his Superior General. Further, he demanded £20 each to pay their passage, plus £12 to reimburse the benevolent whaling captain and another £6 to repay money he had borrowed in Albany. The bishop agreed to all this but insisted on a detailed accounting of expenses. End of round two.

Shortly thereafter, when Thévaux went to Brady with the requested accounting, His Lordship said they could remain in Australia. Thévaux insisted on departing, but was loath to leave Thiersé and Brother Vincent behind. Brady reduced the passage money for each of them from £20 to £15, and voluntarily gave Thévaux power up to the moment of his departure, adding that he was free from all ecclesiastical penalties. End of round three.

Next morning after Mass, in a dramatic scene in the bishop's quarters, Brady threw himself on his knees before Thévaux, lifted his hands to heaven and prayed to God in a loud voice to curse anyone who spoke evil of a bishop, recounting several times the scandal that had occurred. Father Thévaux reassured him that he had no evil intentions and retracted anything that appeared suspect. So ended round four.

The next scene between the two of them should have been their last interaction, as Thévaux was preparing to take his leave. The bishop rushed in and placed all blame on the French priest for not leaving the Sound when he was instructed to do so. Thévaux, however, had heard enough: exasperated, he replied that they had discussed all that the night before and that he would not stand for any further rebuke. Frustrated by his loss, Brady insisted on the last word: 'I have well known that you are off balance and not able to do the job, I was told that at La Neuville, only it was added that you were young, lacking judgement.' End of the fifth round, and, it would seem, the match.

But not quite the final straw: as Thévaux climbed aboard his coach to depart, Joostens arrived with an explosive note from his Lordship: 'Please inform Father Thévaux that his suspension remains because of his disobedience, false witness, and offensive language to his Bishop.'[108] Once again, as he had done at La Neuville with Libermann, and then with Thévaux himself a year earlier as he was departing for Albany, Brady suddenly and without opportunity of discussion or recourse went back on his word to unravel agreements that had already been made.

At the first stop Thévaux wrote to Brady, asking him to lift the suspension and authorise him to hear Thiersé's confession. But Brady would not relent: 'You have had the audacity to insult me personally and before my Vicar General and the college students … it is up to yourself to avoid suspension.'[109] And in a further gesture of vindictiveness, the Bishop cancelled the £16 he had granted the two missionaries for provisions, reducing the men to absolute poverty.

Even before Thévaux had arrived at Perth, the bishop had sought to forestall any difficulties that might arise from the priest's behaviour or as a result of the letters of protest Thévaux had already sent. On 12 March 1847 Brady had written to the Cardinal Prefect of Propaganda to complain about Signor Caporelli, the Benedictines, and Thévaux's mission:

> The Libermann Congregation in no way wishes to establish themselves on land given them by the Government for their use and that of the blacks. They have spent all the money I gave them in the little village of the Sound. They have cost the mission 10,000 francs [he meant no more than 400 francs but, once again, inflated the number, apparently for dramatic effect]. They have done nothing as yet ... They tell me now that they cannot go out on the mission because they are obliged by their Constitutions to live in community, but they could live in the interior, where the blacks are, in community, and at the same time in civilising and converting the aborigines. I have just written to Father Libermann, either send me missionaries with the proper spirit or withdraw those he sent me... He was wrong to send me a young man full of pride, with pretensions to be Superior, and all sick men.[110]

In a letter to Libermann of 19 March 1847, Brady recounted Thévaux's alleged failings: '...disobedience, false reports, and words of harm to religion, and by letters...'[111] But it is noteworthy that he chose never to mention the foundation of Santa Maria at Mollyalup, instituted at his own orders the previous year.

As for replacements, Libermann had apparently considered that, since in a letter of 16 July 1847 Brady thanked him for the anticipated arrival of two priests, one of whom was to replace Father Thévaux.

By the end of August 1847 the replacements still had not arrived, and we can imagine what must have happened: when Libermann had promised reinforcements, he had not yet received the alarming letters from Thévaux and Thiersé written nearly a year earlier. When their letters did arrive in France, in February of 1847, Libermann lost no time in responding to Thévaux and assuring the men that he would submit the whole affair to the Holy See:

I was led in error just like yourself, and there is no way I
could discover it or take means to be better informed… I cannot give you any advice at present. (We await the response
from the Propagation of the Faith.) I gave advice in my last
letter: to examine it before God and carry it out as the Holy
Spirit inspires you. Don't take too literal a view of the advice.
It is up to you to examine it and act accordingly. I had not received your letter of June 1st. If I had, I might, perhaps, have
modified some of the counsels I gave. Have peace of soul always in you and between you all.[112]

This letter, like so many dispatches from the Superior, never
reached the priests at Albany. Under the circumstances, this
may have been for the better, since Thévaux would no doubt
have been troubled by its seeming reproach. In the meantime,
the Fathers had to make their own decision as to the future.
Given the delays in communication, there was no way
Libermann could know that Thévaux had already departed, nor
could the priests know that Libermann agreed whole-heartedly
with their decision and had, in the spring of 1847, sent a letter re-
quiring them to abandon their mission.

When Libermann received Thévaux's and Thiersé's letters,
he had written to Propaganda, asking for permission to withdraw from the mission and citing the reasons: the scarcity of natives and their extreme dispersion, the disproportionate expense
and effort of trekking for miles through the bush to find only
small groups of aborigines, the poverty of the soil, and the con-
stant suffering of the missionaries. He added that saving the
mission would require four priests and a few Brothers: '…their
health would be exhausted in a few years from the unceasing
work and privations they would have to undergo. For such a
difficult mission, men with exceptional qualities would need to
be chosen, only to be sacrificed for little result when they would
be more useful elsewhere.'[113] And he must have foreseen that in
light of the small, widely dispersed population, any subvention
from the Propagation of the Faith would be very modest.

At the time of this writing, Libermann believed that Thiersé had been evacuated from Australia, leaving Thévaux alone. This gave him reason to suggest that the mission at the Sound could be closed with a minimum of public fanfare: 'He [Thévaux] could discreetly leave the mission without harming the Bishop of Perth in the minds of the people; nobody would know we were withdrawing from the mission, and the errors of Bishop Brady would remain unknown.'[114] With characteristic charity, Libermann thus not only refrains from blaming Bishop Brady, but tries to save his face. In the event that the Congregation of the Faith should rule that the mission be maintained, however, Libermann added: '...we think it urgent and indispensable that we alone be in charge. Without that, we feel it would be morally impossible to do the right thing.'[115]

On 19 April 1847 Cardinal Fransoni replied that Libermann should negotiate the withdrawal with Bishop Brady directly since they together had arranged the Australian missions in the first place, adding that the Congregation for the Propagation of the Faith was prepared to accept whatever solution they thought best.

Father Libermann received the Cardinal's directions on 2 May 1847 and wrote immediately to Thévaux, expressing regret but also looking toward the future:

> As soon as you receive this letter, go to Bishop Brady and make arrangements to leave Australia as soon as possible. Go directly to Bourbon or Mauritius. If the Bishop does not pay your passage, you just boldly get on a ship, guaranteeing to pay on arrival in Mauritius or Bourbon ... Should you have any further difficulties regarding your departure, do not consult me ... the distance is too great ... you could perish before you have an answer; seek advice and act according to God's pleasure.[116]

(To keep in mind the effect of postal delays on the unfolding events of this narrative, note that Libermann's letter of 2 May 1847 did not reach Fr Thiersé until January 1848. And Thiersé's reply did not arrive back at Amiens until 31 May 1848. Thus, a complete exchange of letters required some 13 months!)

Thévaux Leaves Australia

Thévaux reached Santa Maria on Easter Sunday, 4 April 1847. Despite what must have been a sad occasion for the missionaries, they began their eight days' retreat that same night.

While Thévaux doubted the validity of his suspension, he at first decided to observe it. 'During the month of April, I felt drawn to join the Third Order of St Francis. The spirit of renunciation I found there and my dire need of it, decided me to enter.'[117] Thiersé had the faculty of admission to the Third Order, and the two young men interpreted literally the provision that admission to the order allowed for a general absolution from all sins and ecclesiastical penalties. And so, from Ascension Day forward, Thévaux recommenced saying Mass, believing in good faith that his suspension was lifted with respect to his priestly powers. However, he abstained from using his jurisdictional powers and did not hear Thiersé's confession for the remainder of his time in Australia.[118]

Meanwhile, Thévaux wrote to Brady to inform him that he was still in Australia because no ship was available. Apparently unsure about the general absolution he had received, he also asked to be absolved from the bishop's censure. Brady responded on 3 June with an insulting and abrasive letter, appointing Thiersé temporary Pro-Vicar Apostolic and granting him power to release Thévaux from the censure if he made amends. The bishop also demanded that the missionaries come to Perth and promised a more hospitable mission in the north. It is obvious that whatever the cost, Brady did not want them to leave the country, fearing the reports they would inevitably make to Rome.

Thiersé's long letter in response (6 June) took a legalistic stance that may seem surprising, but he refused out of hand the position of Pro-Vicar Apostolic and all powers to absolve Thévaux, in the name of the Rule of their Society. Broadly speaking, his argument went as follows: since Thévaux had been appointed Superior by Libermann, only Libermann could replace him; until Libermann appointed another Superior, Thévaux would remain in charge.

Thiersé went on to praise Thévaux for his devotion to the welfare of his confrères and his zeal for the mission. He even challenged the bishop: 'If during all the time you were on the mission you were treated as we were, what would you say?' He told of trekking barefoot for lack of shoes, living off wild plants and stray animals, and perhaps worst of all, the insults from Protestants, which they had endured in silence, such as: *Why did you come to this country? Your bishop is no gentleman, he will never give you a penny. He is no good. What would you say, when the Propaganda money comes [and] your Bishop has money for everyone but you ... he upbraids you for not working the land, even though you didn't come here to cultivate the soil but to save souls.*

Thiersé concludes the letter by explaining that if Thévaux's words were at times strong, or if his demands seemed unreasonable, it was all for the good of the mission: 'I implore Your Eminence, for the honour of Our Saviour, Jesus Christ, not to take offence at what I have written. I do not wish to pain anyone, and since I am only a poor German I never had the leisure to attend a school of politeness. I only wish to obey my Superior. I only know forthrightness, truth, and fairness.'[119]

On 15 July the Fathers learned that a ship was sailing for Mauritius. Even though they had no response from Father Libermann, they made the difficult decision to depart. On 16 July they left the mission of Santa Maria, each with a small bundle of personal items, abandoning the rest to divine Providence. Their journey to Albany involved wading through water up to their armpits, in freezing cold, and gale-force winds. 'The Good God in a marvellous manner provided us with fire when we were almost numb with the cold and soaking wet.' (This was in reference to a tree set on fire by lightning.)

The *Endora* set sail on 22 July, and the men thought they had seen the last of their adopted home. But Australia refused to release its grip: after nine days of contrary winds, the ship was forced to return to port. Once again the departure was attempted, and once again the *Endora* returned to King George Sound.

They had hardly landed when a dying man was brought to them. Some months earlier they had tried to persuade him to return to the practice of his faith and offered him a rosary. He said he didn't need the Rosary devotion, as he could read and write. Thiersé argued that he himself could read and write, but said the beads every day. The man reluctantly took the rosary, saying he would be back to make his confession. The missionaries had sailed without seeing him. Now here he was ready to make his peace with God. 'This is the happiest day of my whole life,' he said. He had worn the beads around his neck and prayed on them several times a day.

When a third attempt to depart failed, and poor Thiersé was so seasick that his life was despaired of, it was decided to leave him at the Sound with Brother Vincent to look after him. On 19 August Thévaux departed alone.

During the long ocean voyage Thévaux began his report on the Australian mission. He completed it at the beginning of October 1847 in Mauritius, and Libermann received the full story in February 1848. Libermann promised to send large extracts to Propaganda so that '...they be made aware of what happened. I will not cover up your errors, and I will tone down Bishop Brady's as best I can.'[120]

Brady's Response

It will be remembered that Thévaux and Thiersé knew nothing of Libermann's plan to send them reinforcements, one of whom was to replace Thévaux as Superior. Once Thévaux had departed for Mauritius on 19 August 1847, Brady wrote two letters to Libermann, characterising the missionaries' departure as a flight: 'I regret I gave them money to go... When I notified them to await the arrival of the new Fathers, they hurried their departure

and asked for more money, of which, happily, I had none.'[121]
The same day, he repeated these untruths to the Secretary of
Propaganda:

> I wish to forewarn Your Eminence of the conduct of l'Abbé
> Thévaux, who, having learned that his Superior in France,
> Father Libermann, had appointed another in his place (and
> at my request), has left the Sound with his companions for
> *Isle de France* [Mauritius], saying he planned to complain that
> his ecclesiastical powers had been suspended and that he
> had been left without temporal help, even though he had
> money to pay sea passage for himself and two others. I am
> obliged to point out that l'Abbé Thévaux is a sly priest, a
> hypocrite and liar, full of pride, *speciem pietatem habens, vir-*
> *tutem negans*… Since they have neither health nor the will to
> do good, I do not regret their departure…[122]

Just before his departure, Thévaux had written one final time to
the bishop to ask his pardon and admit all his faults. On 15
September Brady wrote to Libermann to announce this last act
of contrition:

> But why didn't he await the arrival of the other Fathers? *A*
> *tout péche misércorde* [no offence is utterly unpardonable] … I
> wish to put the case in your hands, Monsieur Superior; *Tibi*
> *soli datur facultas tollendi suspensionem qua inodatus est a nostro*
> *Vicario Genarali positis ponendi*… He knew that you had ap-
> pointed another head of the community. It is all over now …
> he left and left with the whole Congregation. Good bye,
> Monsieur le Superior, you will be the judge.[123]

Effectively, Brady now had only the Sisters, Father Joostens, and
the two Benedictines – Serra and Salvado, with whom he was at
open warfare. In 1848 and '49 both Serra and Salvado were
made bishops and Joostens departed for Batavia (Dutch East
Indies). In short order, Brady found himself alone.

Thévaux, Thiersé and Brother Vincent

Libermann had serious doubts about the validity of lifting Thévaux's suspension, so he wrote to Cardinal Fransoni on 9 April 1848 to explain the case: 'I am persuaded that these errors arise from ignorance of canon law which is greatly neglected in the French seminaries.' On 10 May, Propaganda, without judging the validity of the suspension since Thévaux had removed himself from the jurisdiction of Bishop Brady, gave Libermann the faculty to absolve Thévaux or to delegate this authority. Since Libermann had no way of knowing just where Thévaux was, he delegated the powers of absolution and dispensation to Laval in Mauritius and to Le Vavasseur in Réunion (Bourbon).[124]

We have left Thiersé with Brother Vincent at King George Sound while Thévaux was sailing for Mauritius. I think that on all sides they were rather pleased with this mishap which put off the need to make decisions about the future, for they were not at ease about sailing all together. Would Libermann approve? To leave like this, on their own accord, was it not a kind of disobedience? In fact, after his suspension on 16 March Thévaux related his interview with the bishop and its outcome and asked Libermann for permission to leave. Even though Bishop Brady had given him some money for leaving with his companions, Libermann thought Thévaux had been '…guileless enough not to dare leave without having permission from me. I am profoundly distressed by this. In such a serious situation, and not having received any news from me, he should have assumed the authorisation and should have left.'[125]

Thévaux and Thiersé had devised a plan for saving the mis-

sion, presuming that the Vicariate Apostolic would be under the
full jurisdiction of the Congregation. Libermann responded cau-
tiously:

> I will advise Propaganda of your proposed plan which you
> believe is the only way to achieve the salvation of the mis-
> sion. I will not ask what we will send to carry out that plan,
> nor will I say that we do not wish to go there; I will content
> myself with expressing my feelings on the subject. Should
> Propaganda tell us to go there, we will accept; in that case I
> would consider it the will of God, even though seemingly
> less prudent. If Propaganda says nothing, I will regard that
> silence as God's will and will give no further thought to
> Australia.[126]

But the only person left at the Sound to carry out any plan was
Thiersé, now fully recovered and still in the company of Brother
Vincent. Thévaux had left him 300 francs, but Brother Vincent
was in rags and needed to be clothed. As for Thiersé, the soutane
would still suffice, for a while, to cover him from head to toe. He
remembered the strange prophecy of Bouchet, that it was he
who would be left to spend some time alone with the natives.
And in a letter to his friend Father Schwindenhammer, he ex-
tolled the bounty of divine Providence in providing for them in
their darkest hours, nourishing and supporting them as it had
the saints of old. But he knew he could not rely on the funds
Thévaux had promised to send once he reached Mauritius, and
Brother Vincent was no longer up to the physical demands of
the wild countryside.

Then, on 24 October 1847 came the first of Libermann's letters to actually reach its destination in Australia, announcing his
intention to submit to Propaganda the difficulties the missionaries had encountered. It proved that the Venerable Father had not
forgotten them.

Thiersé replied immediately, reporting that he had again
taken on the mission. He wanted to return to Santa Maria, ad-
mitting that he was '…nearly content to stay there: I liked these
poor people very much, despite their poor qualities.'[127] And

while he suffered the calumnies of Protestants who '...suspected our morals and accused us of eating candles,'[128] he experienced great graces.

Despite two letters to Brady, he reported, he had not yet received an answer, and he wondered if he still had faculties, in light of the fact that he had left the mission during the three abortive attempts to set sail. Finally, he reported the joy of receiving letters from Fathers Le Vavasseur, Collin, Laval and Lambert, plus a bank draft for 1,000 francs – of no value to him, apparently, since it was drafted on a bank in Adelaide some 3,000 miles away.

On 18 January 1848 Thiersé received Libermann's letter of the previous May, recalling the missionaries. 'That news distressed me greatly because I saw the most miserable of all peoples being abandoned entirely to the fury of the devil... I would stay on ... in Australia one could have a departure point for New Guinea and the other islands of Oceania, where there are so many black people and so few priests, if any at all.'[129]

Thiersé went on to explain the difficulties that had prevented his departure: lack of funds, the departure of the French whaling fleet for the coast of Russia (later Thiersé would actually consider taking passage on one of these whaling ships and returning to France on foot!), and the fact that there was only one ship each year for Mauritius, and passage had to be paid in advance. In conclusion, he announced his intention to remain and await instructions from Libermann once the situation had been reviewed.

He also gave an account of his ministry: in six months he had confessed 10 people, given the last sacraments to a man, baptised one woman, and given instructions to two Protestants. He also spoke of the kindness of one Lawrence Mooney, an Irish veteran soldier at King George Sound:

This wonderful man with his wife and children had already given me a sack of flour and has lent me another and now he has come to me with 25 francs and told me if he was not so poor with his seven children that he would have liked to give

10 times as much. This poor fellow has had to endure hunger along with his whole family in order to help me. You know how hard it is for me to take anything from them. They give all the money they can, and in their charity, never fail to find something for me. When I arrived from the bush I was half dead, for I had only a little bread, four potatoes and three eggs to carry me through my journey of ten days. A mother could not have cared for her children better than that family looked after me. They all slept on the floor in order to give me a decent bed. As I was in the grip of a fever I was forced to accept their offer and remain there ten days. Tomorrow I will start again on another trip into the bush, but I won't be as sick going as I was arriving, for the same family has given me a bottle of brandy, and the wife has given me a pie, a few herrings and several eggs.[130]

But still there persisted bad blood with Bishop Brady. For eight months Brady refused to forward a box sent by Libermann and intended for the mission at the Sound. The bishop also turned a deaf ear to a request for Mass wine and a bit of tobacco. 'However,' wrote Thiersé, 'if he should try to treat me as he treated Father Thévaux or decide to give us nothing, I will go to Adelaide or Sydney. But do not think that we are sorry to be here. Even after I leave, if you wish me to return, I will begin again.'[131]

In a letter of 14 June 1848 Thiersé appears near the breaking point: 'It appears that the Bishop has determined to let us die from hunger and misery.'[132] Brady had given him faculties and grand promises, but nothing to live on. On one of his last treks Thiersé collapsed from weakness and lay down under a tree to die. Revived by neighbouring farmers, he returned to Santa Maria and wrote to Brady about his condition, begging for alms. Eventually he was able to take possession of the box sent by Libermann and sold it to obtain credit on Le Vavasseur's bank draft. Perhaps most disheartening, despite all Thévaux's promises, no word came from Mauritius.

The End of The Mission

Life for Thiersé and Brother Vincent that year was a struggle for survival, a daily search for food to live on. For five months they lived on nothing but wild ducks and other fowl.

At the beginning of Lent we had nothing left, neither powder nor shot to hunt, nor provisions. We had begun a novena to St Joseph, when we were alerted that there was a parcel left for us about three miles away; it contained three bottles of wine, a few pounds of butter, 20 pounds of pork, and a pound of candles. That was the fifth time this happened to us. It was the good Catholic policeman of King George Sound who thought of us again. He even gave his policeman's riding coat, which the Governor had given him... Without food, nothing can be done here.[133]

But the two men realised that their position was untenable in the long term. In the spring they found a ship sailing for Mauritius, which they reached in September 1848. The poor missionary's appearance when he arrived showed beyond doubt how destitute he was. A local paper, *Le Pays*, recalled the occasion: 'Everyone remembers the lamentable state he was in on his arrival; he had for baggage a well-worn bonnet – a present from a sailor, and a tailcoat full of holes – a token of the generosity of a Provincial Governor.'[134]

Epilogue

Bishop Brady's mounting debts eventually forced him to appeal to Europe for help. As emissary he decided to send Serra, the Benedictine, who departed on 20 February 1848. Serra was greeted by revolution on the continent, but while he had some success in raising funds, Rome had other plans for him. At the request of Archbishop Polding of Sydney, the Congregation of the Faith decided to erect Port Essington (the former mission of Don Confalonieri) into a diocese, with the name 'Port Victoria,' for which Dom Serra was named bishop and consecrated on 15 August 1848.

Not surprisingly, this turn of events caused great consternation in Perth. Brady hastened to send Dom Salvado, the second Benedictine, to continue the appeal. To avoid being left without any priest, in early January 1849 the bishop promptly ordained Timothy Donovan – the first ordination in Western Australia.

Salvado received a shock when he presented himself at the headquarters of the Society of the Propagation of the Faith: he was asked the question, 'The Society of the Propagation of the Faith has sent Dr Brady 144,710 francs for his mission. He tells us he spent 11,000; what has he done with the other 133,710?'[135] The cardinals of the Propaganda would have to investigate, and Salvado returned to his monastery at La Cava, near Naples.

In the meantime Bishop Brady had appealed to Rome for a Coadjutor to help sort out his financial affairs. He expected Salvado but instead got Serra, who, as bishop of Port Victoria, had far more resources in money and men. From the beginning, Brady and Serra never got on. By early 1850 Brady set off for Rome to register a complaint about his Coadjutor, but there was more than one voice to be heard on the matter: Salvado was still available as a first-hand witness to the Australian misadventure, and Cardinal Fransoni invited him to give a detailed account.

As a result, Brady was placed under interdict not to return to Australia. When he returned anyway, he was automatically suspended. At last, having failed in his attempt to take proceedings against Serra, Brady finally returned to Ireland, to Castletara, County Cavan. Despite poor health he took part in Vatican I, and after the Council he moved to Amelie-Les-Bains, a hot mineral spa in the eastern Pyrenees specialising in the treatment of rheumatism. And it was here, on 3 December 1871, that Bishop Brady died at the age of 82, intestate and apparently in penury, though it was later revealed that he had deposits in French and English banks.[136]

In a letter to Cardinal Fransoni dated 26 August 1852, Archbishop Polding reported that all of Brady's property in Australia had been transferred to the diocese of Perth:

> ...I regret to add that the Rev Dr Brady did not persevere in the good dispositions which are manifested in the Document signed by him on the Altar. This he has endeavoured to set aside in a court of law, but in vain – the Document being admitted as valid, and legal purposes binding, by a decision of the judge in the Colonial jurisdiction. These proceedings on the part of Bishop Brady incline me to believe that he is devoid of Religious and honourable principle or he is not of sane mind.[137]

Libermann's Last Word

Libermann never revealed to the Holy See the rough treatment his missionaries had experienced at the hands of Bishop Brady. He accepted Thévaux's suspension as something to be kept private, pledging his men to cede almost everything except community life. And while he did submit large extracts of Thévaux's report, he declined to editorialise: 'But I make no comment. Your Excellency will judge according to the wisdom of the spirit of God therein, and we will accept with respect whatever advice or reprimand we will merit.'[138]

Making no accusations against Brady, Libermann spoke only of the shortcomings of Thévaux. The Bendictines (who had less to suffer from the bishop), on the contrary, did not spare him, accused him bluntly, and finally got rid of him. But Libermann never added fuel to their fire. For him the Australian venture ended in 1847 and 1848, and there was no further reason to return to it.

For his two missionaries from the Sound, Libermann had a final message.

To Thévaux, the fiery, obstinate character, who sometimes lacked flexibility and discretion, he made the following thoughtful rebuke:

> You have, perhaps, too much tendency to fasten on matters of less importance. You did well to hold on to the essential rule of two together and not allow an outsider to control community life. You didn't keep sufficiently calm and cool; you allowed yourself to be irritated too much … many mistakes occur when one is in an upset state. I hope you will learn to profit from all that. No matter what injustices are inflicted on us, our soul must remain calm before God. Above all, we must avoid speaking and acting when we feel ourselves getting agitated. Perhaps and probably, there is too much rigidity in your words and actions. It is a fault of yours that you have to be on guard against generally suffering has taught you a lot of things and the necessity to review the past, the reflection on which would help you get a better understanding of things and see your mistakes more clearly. What remains is to place everything in the hands of God to correct whatever may be imperfect in your soul.[139]

For Fr Thiersé, a more conciliatory word:

> I hope the consolations that will be given you in caring for the dear Blacks in Mauritius will be compensation for the fruitless Australian situation; and the sufferings you endured there will fructify your work …[140]

For Fr Libermann everything was grace! The Australian experience was indeed a purifying experience for the two missionaries, and one which prepared them for their great apostolate in Mauritius. It was this thought that Thiersé himself captured so well when he wrote to Libermann from King George Sound: 'I will remain voluntarily in this poor land, should you wish so, for this [Australian] mission has this good: that, like it or not, penance must be done and pure charity exercised, at the mercy of the Good Lord.'[141]

Mauritius Epilogue

The Island of Mauritius lies 550 miles east of Madagascar in the Indian Ocean. It comprises only 720 square miles, being some 36 miles long and 26 miles wide. In 1846, about the time Thévaux and Thiersé arrived, the island's population totalled 158,462–102,217 general population (African and Coloured), and 56,245 Indian. Eleven years earlier, in 1835, more than 63,000 slaves had been emancipated. The few clergy took care of the whites and coloured people, while the former slaves rarely received any religious instruction at all. It was these blacks that Frs Laval, Thévaux, and Thiersé targeted as their special apostolate – *La Mission des Noirs*.

The mission had begun on 14 September 1841 with the arrival of Fr Laval, the first Holy Heart of Mary missionary. Five months later Laval sent the following account to Fr Libermann of the situation facing him:

> Corruption and licentiousness are unbelievable. There are some 80,000 blacks on the Island; I am the only one to care for them. Half of them are not baptised; those who are live like pagans. Very few of them have been married in church. They leave and return to each other several times. They are given to drunkenness. All the young black girls are objects for debauchery by their masters or by young white Mauritians. Blacks born on the Island, called Creoles, are corrupt. I try to deal with a few poor Malgaches and Mozambicans.[142]

On his arrival in 1847, under conditions which cannot have improved much, Thévaux threw himself heart and soul into the work. In a letter of 21 January 1849 to l'Abbé Gamon, Libermann sang his praises: 'Fr Thévaux is working with Fr Laval in Mauritius, doing marvellously. Chapels are being erected as if by a miracle; to date there are more than twenty of them, each a foyer of grace which attracts people and leads them to conversion.'[143]

These chapels were simple constructions of bamboo with a thatched roof, mostly built by the converts, each chapel having its own catechist. Later on more solid buildings were built. In the meantime they were crucial in Laval's and his fellow missionaries' strategy in converting the rural areas. 'The numerous chapels of Fr Laval were foyers of light which spread the faith to the most backward areas of the Island.'[144]

The fruit of that approach was prodigious. 'I think there is no country in the world where doing good is so well prepared and the harvest so great,' wrote Thévaux.[145] At the end of 1847 Frs Laval, Thévaux and Lambert passed four to eight hours per day in the confessional, hearing about 8,000 confessions per month. And in 1848 Thévaux reported to Father Libermann, 'Happy ministry. It bore fruit in abundance!'[146]

The newspapers of the Island, *Le Cerneen* and *Le Pays*, were later to pay tribute to Thévaux's work. For 30 years several parishes successively experienced his apostolic zeal and devotion to souls. Always on foot, nothing defeated him. He covered all areas – arranging meetings, organising catechism classes, building chapels and churches. His work was immense. Early on Sunday mornings he would say Mass in Bambous, 15 or 16 miles from Port Louis, the capital, and then return to the city to preach at the eleven o'clock Mass. Later, Bishop Collier sent him to Pamplemousses, where his zeal was such that he had to enlarge the church to cater to an ever growing flock. He also ministered in several other churches throughout the island.

Thévaux on the Island of Rodrigues

Early in December 1850 Thévaux became the first Catholic priest in 90 years to set foot on Rodrigues, a small island 342 miles east of Mauritius. At the time the island had a population of only

500–350 natives, Africans or Malgaches, and 150 Mauritian
Creoles. The latter lived at Port-Mathurin, a small fishing centre;
the other peoples lived inland at Saint-Gabriel, in the moun-
tains.

For years the people of Rodrigues had been asking for a
priest. They were born, they lived, and they died without the
benefits or consolation of religion. But it was practically impossible to send a priest without the consent of the Governor.
However, as luck would have it, in 1850 the Anglican
Archbishop of Colombo, Ceylon, who had just spent a few
months in Mauritius, expressed his desire to visit the Seychelles.
For this he received a grant of £150 from the Colonial Office. As
a consequence, Governor George Anderson, more liberal than
his predecessors, obtained a £50 grant from the Colonial
Secretary to send a Catholic missionary to Rodrigues.

In the five months he was there Thévaux built two chapels,
one at Port-Mathurin and one at Saint-Gabriel, but his main
work was catechising: he baptised 288, blessed 53 marriages,
and admitted 24 people to first communion. He installed a catechist in each chapel to preside at prayers on Sundays and feast
days and to instruct as best they could during the week. In April
1851 Thévaux returned to Mauritius and presented a report to
the civil authorities and a more detailed one to Fr Libermann (20
June 1851). The two catechists carried on until the next priest,
Father J.B. François CSSp, arrived in 1856. He left in May of 1857
and returned later the same year with Bishop Collier, which
marked the beginning of a regular episcopal visitation.[147]

But the physical demands of the mission took their toll:
Thévaux continued to suffer with a diseased leg which had
bothered him since he left Australia. Although several doctors
advised amputation, Laval, himself a doctor, had a different
opinion. Thévaux was willing to do whatever his superior decided. He asked Laval how long before he could be better.
'Twelve months,' replied Laval. 'It's too long,' said Thévaux,
'Better amputate... I could not spend twelve months not working for God.'[148] However, after Laval assured him that he could

partly exercise his ministry while convalescing, he accepted. The knee was ankylosed but remained stiff, and so Thévaux had to return to Port Louis, much to his regret. He took on light charitable work and his ministry again proved very successful. He became chaplain to a convent of the Filles de Marie (Daughters of Mary) in Port Louis and founded schools for the poor, both in the city and in St-Croix parish on the city outskirts. When the saintly Laval died in 1864, Thévaux became chaplain to the prisons.

Before his death, Father Laval gave a unique view of Thévaux's character when a Father Buguel, newly arrived in the colony [8 December 1855], asked him what special advice he could give with regard to his new superior:

> Pray a lot to God and our good Mother and then be in agreement with Fr Thévaux. If sometimes you find him a little severe, a bit exacting with respect to the formalities, pardon him, because he is a holy man and can give you good advice … in all things count on God alone! Then if it should happen, as it happens to everybody, that you do something stupid, dear confrère, don't get discouraged, pull yourself up at once and calmly go on with your work without being disheartened. Only proud and silly people get discouraged because of their faults, because they are not aware of their own weakness. If they knew what our poor hearts are really like, they would be surprised at only one thing, that is, that they do not fall more often and more drastically.[149]

Thévaux Returns to France

In 1866 Thévaux returned to France for several months of well-deserved holiday. Back in Mauritius in 1867 he was warmly welcomed, but he found Port Louis in the grip of widespread cholera. More than half the population had succumbed to the disease, and the city resembled a vast hospital.

Thévaux gave himself unstintingly, an example to all. The visits to the sick were so organised that practically no Catholic died without the sacraments. The other priests had the consolation of baptising a goodly number of pagans and received many

Protestants into the church, converted by the touching example of the devotion of the missionaries. In the end, Thévaux caught the fever and was forced to rest. He responded to the great care he got and was soon back to his ministry.[150]

In 1862 Thévaux had, against his own wishes, been appointed Provincial Superior. He humbly pointed out his faults and defects in a letter to the Superior General, Father Schwindenhammer:

> Another reason for my desire to be discharged from all superiorship is that for some time now I feel strongly attracted to the spirit of prayer and union with Our Lord. Since my last sicknesses, the good Lord has given me many graces. He draws me to Himself so strongly I have such desire and satisfaction in prayer that I wish to do that only. If I were permitted I would voluntarily withdraw to a desert where I would only have to love and contemplate Our Lord... that attraction has lasted nearly a year now.[151]

When he was finally released from his duties as Provincial in 1872, Thévaux poured out his soul in thanks, asking forgiveness for any faults he committed during his long tenure. The appointment of the new Superior led to a widespread rumour that Thévaux was leaving Mauritius, and the local papers published articles praising him and regretting his departure from the colony. Thévaux wrote, 'I spent two weeks denying the rumour.'[152]

From early in 1876 Thévaux developed a severe throat infection which forced him to relinquish most of his ministry. In August that year, under doctor's orders, he set sail for Bourbon (Réunion Island), where the change of climate was hoped to improve his condition. As for himself, Thévaux placed himself completely in the hands of God, very grateful for the wonderful support he got from his confrères and his many friends.

When he returned from Bourbon, it was arranged that he should recuperate at St André, a country house owned by his great friend, Mr Jules Langlois, who put a pavilion at the priest's disposal. Here Thévaux had an oratory where he could say Mass, and two Sisters of Charity to look after him. But away from his beloved Port Louis he felt out of his element, and on 14 January 1877 he attempted to return. A recurring fever forced him to retreat to St André, where on 19 January, his strength failing, he called for his Superior, Fr Guilloux. 'I feel that this is the end,' he said, 'I have arrived at the point where Fr Laval was.' 'As for the rest,' he continued in a voice still firm, 'I am not afraid of death... I am ready.'[153]

> The dear Father remained conscious up to 10 o'clock in the evening; only a short while before, he consented to leave his chair to lie on the bed. From then on he weakened more and more, and passed away without suffering, without pain, in the arms of Fr Jouan, in the peace of the Lord, towards midnight of 20 or 21 January. He was 57 years old.[154]

> On Monday 22 January the obsequies took place in Port Louis Cathedral presided over by Bishop Scarisbrick midst a vast crowd. After the ceremony his body was transported to Saint Coeur de Marie Church, Petite-Riviere to be buried with Father Baud and Father Lambert, in a tomb erected by 'grateful and sorrowing parishioners.'[155]

Fr Thiersé 1848–1880

Arriving in Mauritius in September 1848, after the long sea voyage from King George Sound and still wearing his tattered coat, Thiersé received a warm welcome from Father Laval.

There was much for him to do: immediately he was assigned to youth work in the Cathedral parish and soon took on the additional responsibilities of Bursar. Thiersé was a faithful correspondent, especially with annual reports to the Superior General in Paris. In one letter he recounts his daily schedule:

> I arise at 4 a.m. and 15 minutes later I begin my morning prayer in church. At 4.55 I lead the faithful in morning prayer. That is followed by Mass and thanksgiving to 6.15 a.m. when I take a break if I have not to bring communion to the sick. I say the little hours of the breviary followed by a short scripture reading, but this is not every day; 6.45 a.m. I hear confessions until 8 a.m. when I breakfast. Afterwards, I

shop for next day's provisions as bursar. At 9 a.m. until 1 p.m. I hear confessions followed by my particular examination of conscience, dinner and recreation or a visit to the sick. At 3 p.m. I return to the confessional until 4.30 p.m. when I hold my daily catechising class. This is followed by confessions from 5.30 p.m. to 7.30 p.m. Unless there is a sick person to visit I then say my Office for the day, supper is at 8.15 p.m.; bed time at 9.45 unless we have a sick call. I have spent whole nights on these calls, for there are many sick. All convert readily. Once you tell them they are children of God, they ask, 'Now can I go to heaven?' When you say yes, they respond, 'Thanks be to God, at this hour I can't ever offend God.' They die happy as angels. You can realise now, dear Father, that with people like this one cannot ever be tired. Only on Sundays do I feel a bit tired.

Every Sunday about 3 a.m. I leave for Petite-Riviere, over 3 miles from the city. There the first chapel was built by Fr Laval and dedicated to the Holy Heart of Mary. Arriving at dawn I hear confessions until 8 a.m. Then Mass, catechetical instruction, followed by baptisms. When I finish, I get on my donkey and return to Port Louis to give instruction at 11.30 a.m. At 3 in the afternoon an hour's catechetical instruction for the young Devotees of Our Lady. At 4 p.m. Vespers and Benediction. Then a meeting with the old people for recitation of the rosary, which has a great influence on them. All these exercises take place in the chapel of Our Lady of the Seven Dolours, which I so love. Finally, at 7 p.m. I sing Vespers in the Cathedral and Fr Baud and myself on alternative Sundays teach catechism.[156]

In 1856 Laval appointed Thiersé parish priest of Grand-Port, where he was to spend most of his career. It was a vast parish. Writing to his Superior General, Laval pointed out '...that to look after so immense a parish would need three priests. I hesitated for a moment if we should take on this charge, but we had to give way since the bishop had nobody to appoint there and one could not leave such a huge parish without care.'[157]

Thiersé was familiar with Grand-Port because he had worked there in 1851 at the request of Fr James Henry, an Irishman and parish priest of Mahebourg, the old capital in the southeast of the island. The parish perimeter stretched for 40 miles, and one needed strong legs and a good mount for places that were nearly impassable. Father Henry had described the parishioners as being '...in deplorable ignorance of religion, and the Blacks were completely neglected.'[158] (Father Henry's predecessor in Grand-Port, Father J.F. Kennelly, another Irishman stationed there from 1847 to 1850, had disappeared one night and left the island without a word to anyone, apparently in despair at the conditions he faced.)

Thiersé described the parish as '...the citadel of the devil... In the beginning I could only spend nine days a month there. However I have the utmost confidence that Our Lady will chase him away. She has done a lot already.'[159] He also paints a vivid picture of the real physical dangers he faced:

Without the help of our Heavenly Queen I would have been certainly drowned on one of my trips. To go to Vieux-Port I had to cross an inlet of the sea six miles wide. One day, when I was crossing, a terrible storm burst upon us right in the middle of our passage. My two boatmen, little skilled in manoeuvring, were not able to stave off a sudden surge of the sea, which landed us on a rock. Fairly heavy damage resulted from the terrible shock. The boat filled with water in the flash of an eye; we were lost, if by superhuman efforts we had not been able to block the hole and bail out the water... But I am always happy to suffer a little, that souls be saved, and I would be glad to give my life if I saw beforehand confrères coming to complete the work begun.[160]

Thiersé Returns to France (1853–1854)

The incessant labours in Australia and Mauritius finally took their toll on the zealous missionary. 'I feel very weak...' he wrote in a letter on 23 April 1853, '...instead of taking rest, I do it again more vigorously.'[161] But there was little hope of recovery in Mauritius, and it was decided that he return to Europe for a complete rest. He went first to Bourbon, where in early May 1853 he took ship for France, accompanied by Collin, the Principal Superior of the communities of Mauritius and Bourbon.

When Thiersé arrived at the Mother House in Paris, he learned of the death of his younger brother, Jean-Baptiste Thiersé, whom he brought to the noviciate. Jean had been sent to West Africa but returned home in February 1853 with serious stomach trouble. When Father François first learned of his brother's illness, he wrote to him: 'Frankly, I was not disturbed when I heard of your illness; because I thought it to be the quickest way for you to go to heaven... Did we not, the two of us, promise Our Lady when we said goodbye at Marienthal that we were prepared to sacrifice everything for Her sake? We must not backtrack now but go forward with the Good Lord.'[162] But Jean-Baptiste had returned to his family in Alsace to convalesce, and he died before he could read these words.

From Paris Thiersé went on to do his retreat with his confréres in Amiens, at Notre-Dame du Gard, an old Cistercian Abbey founded in 1137 and acquired by Libermann in 1846 to cater to his ever growing numbers of theology and philosophy students. Thiersé was delighted to see the progress.

The missionary's next stop was home, where he regaled his family and friends with tales of his experiences. The parish priest of Mulhouse, M. Uhlemann, recorded of this visit: 'Behold, in my opinion a real missionary; what colossal faith, what simplicity. Oh, how he edified and enthralled us.'[163]

Before returning to Mauritius in 1854, Thiersé received permission from the Superior General and his Council for his confrères to seek British citizenship. This was very important for the permanency of their mission: Father Laval had been on his own for nearly five years, with no confrère permitted to join him until Father Lambert arrived in December 1846, Father Thévaux in October 1847, and Father Thiersé in September 1848.

This was during the hostile governorship of Sir William

Gomm (1842-1848), who in his dispatches to the Colonial Office never ceased to present those priests as a grave danger to the colony:

> ...prudent, not revealing their hand, they are the agents of the French Government, paid to turn the mass of the people against British institutions. The black population seem loyal enough to the Crown, but hypothetically should the English and the French clash over control of the colony, it wouldn't be astonishing to see a considerable section of that population change their allegiance away from her Majesty.[164]

Lord Gray, a member of the Liberal Party and at that time Colonial Secretary, replied: '...as long as their conduct is above board and they conform to police regulations, they should be permitted to live in the colony.'[165] Despite this assurance, however, Laval in a letter to Libermann (October 1847) remarked: 'As long as we are French or other non-nationals, we will always be uneasy and never free.'[166]

In addition to this estrangement, Libermann faced another worry: Laval was the only man who received a government salary-which would hardly suffice to support four priests. If anything happened to Laval, the mission would have to close. The solution to the problem was for the missionaries to become British subjects, but this was much easier said than done, not least of all because of the tensions that persisted, even in the case of Thiersé.[167]

Thiersé Returns to Mauritius (1854)

Father Thiersé sailed from Bordeaux on 13 January and arrived in Port Louis, Mauritius on 5 May. News of his arrival spread like wildfire, and so many people gathered at the dockside that he could hardly force his way through. 'For two days,' he wrote in a letter of 13 May, 'I could do nothing accept to say "bonjour, bonjour" continually. It was a procession from morning to night. Everybody was delighted; the only words to be heard were (in the local patois) "Grand merci, bon Die, le père li fini veni, c'est la Ste Vierge qui amene li; nous si bien plore quand li parti; á cet' heure la nous contents, contents même."'[168]

(Thanks to the Good Lord, Father has come back, it is Our Lady's doing; we who cried so much when he departed now are very happy he is back, very happy indeed.)

But the air of celebration was soon cancelled by an outbreak of cholera. In a letter of 4 August 1854 Thiersé described the horrific scene:

> The city of Port Louis would rend your heart; nothing was to be heard except weeping and wailing and the sombre rumble of carts hauling away the dead. But what numbers were brought back to the Good God! The churches were never closed from early morning to late at night; many married in good health in the morning were in the cemetery by evening. All shops and stores closed; on the streets you met nobody but people looking for a doctor or priest ... without the strength of the Good Lord, the pain and anguish I suffered at what I saw might have caused my death.[169]

After a short break, the cholera gave way to smallpox, with the same dire consequences. 'Unworthy we were to shed our blood as martyrs, we became instead martyrs of charity... Every day we offer the Good God the sacrifice of our lives; nevertheless, I pray Our Saviour to let me live until the epidemic ceases and there are enough confrères to do the needful.'[170]

Parish Priest of Grand-Port/Mahebourg

In 1856 Father Henry, parish priest of Grand-Port/Mahebourg, retired. Appointed as his successor, Thiersé took up permanent residence in what became his special apostolic field for the next 23 years. The Catholics at that time numbered about 8,000 and were scattered over a vast area, miles from Mahebourg town, which itself hardly contained half the parish. Thiersé gave some idea of the labour involved in a letter of 1867: 'Yesterday I travelled 11 leagues, partly by sea and partly on foot in torrential rain, to see three sick people, and those journeys are not infrequent.'[171] Because of their distance from a church, most of the parishioners were unable to attend Mass or religious instruction. Moreover, the church at Mahebourg scarcely held 600 people. In 1850, when Thiersé first ministered in the parish, of 8,000 Catholics only 100 frequented the sacraments.[172]

Matters began to change when Laval's well-tried method of evangelisation was set up, with admirable results: in every area Thiersé started to gather together small groups who were well-disposed to receive instruction. That led to others joining and initially to the construction of a small chapel where Mass was said. In a few years 16 chapels were erected – first mere straw huts, as he called them, and gradually more solid buildings of stone and wood.

Thiersé arranged that in the principal churches – Notre Dame de Refuge, St Patrice, and St François – Xavier-Sunday Mass was said and instruction given. During the week the smaller chapels (including St Philomene, Notre Dame du Bon Secours, Notre Dame des Sept Douleurs, Le Sacré Coeur, St Elisabeth and St Anne, among others) were used for catechising and hearing confessions. To list that number of sacred foundations alone gives an idea of the extent of Thiersé's labours. Even so, it should be noted that during his 23-year tenure in the parish he often worked alone or with the assistance of two other priests, while the population called for three times that number.

Fr Thiersé's Charity

The area of Mahebourg was cruelly visited by poverty, famine, and epidemics in the late 1860s, as well as by cyclones in 1868 and 1874, and by dengue fever in 1872. Of this outbreak of dengue Thiersé recounted, 'We have over 10,000 people sick with fever. We need to find medicine and food, people cannot work any longer, there is nobody in most of the houses who can give a glass of water to others; each day I need a flagon of quinine and 200 biscuits, not to mention other things.'[173]

His door was always open to the poor. The local newspapers paid this tribute to him: 'While the fever raged, one can say that wherever there was any one sick, Father was there. Doctors avowed that they never visited the sick but Fr Thiersé had already been there before them. It seemed he had the gift of ubiquity.'[174]

Catholic Schools Established

While the six government schools were well-funded and supported an enrolment of 250 pupils, the Catholic schools were left to their own devices to teach 120 pupils. Thiersé first opened a school for girls and an orphanage supervised by the Daughters of Mary. These were followed by other schools for boys highly praised for their academic standards, so that by 1874 1,000 pupils were receiving Christian education. 'To bring these enterprises to fruition required all the indomitable courage and perseverance of Thiersé. When it came to schools no difficulties would impede him.'[175]

Mission to South Africa

In 1870 the Vicar-Apostolic of Capetown, Bishop Grimley, wrote to the Superior General of the Holy Ghost Fathers, Fr Schwindenhammer, requesting that he take over a sizeable section of his territory which at that time had no priests whatsoever. Since Thiersé spoke English, the Superior General asked him to go the Cape to report on the situation. No doubt Thiersé recalled his first visit there in November 1845 and thought it would be good place to open a mission. He arrived in South Africa in December 1870. Though his report was excellent, outlining the pros and cons objectively, the Mother House ultimately declined the offer; they believed it would be impossible to observe community life there and they lacked the personnel to staff such a mission in view of their commitments elsewhere in Africa.

A Final Portrait of Fr Thiersé

Thiersé's long-time friend and early Superior, Father Thévaux, is perhaps best-suited to give a faithful portrait of this selfless missionary:

> Father Thiersé is always the good and valiant missionary, full of zeal and ardour for the salvation of souls. Years, weariness, sickness – nothing can temper his enduring zeal. He is always the holy man, full of God's love, with a delicate conscience, a good religious, a lover of the Rule, faithful in keeping it. I find only that he is a little exaggerated in certain things, at least in how he behaves.[176]

He had, in other words, the defects of his virtues. Thiersé himself would be the first to admit his faults and was always grateful to have them brought to his attention. He was always open
and frank with his superiors. He wrote an annual letter to the
Superior General, rendering an account of his year and humbly
seeking advice. He took a keen interest in all matters concerning
the Congregation. 'I get great pleasure,' he wrote, 'in reading the
General Bulletin, when I see the considerable growth in the
numbers of scholastics and novices. May the Good Lord bless
our little society and make it fructify for the glory of God and the
salvation of souls. That is my overwhelming desire. As for us,
we will economise as much as possible to help our Mother-
House, for we all love it like a child loves his mother.'[177]

Thiersé's trials and difficulties manifest his deep faith, his
humility, and his generosity:

The suffering, the crosses, the insults and the outrages lav-
ished upon me all too often, in Grand-Port, no longer upset
me; I keep calm when I am not to blame; I experience in that
situation a sense of indifference... God blesses my ministry.
If I could only pray and was not so sinful, I would be the happiest man in the world. For those two things I cannot but
weep before God and rely only on his divine mercy... I always like doing the work, no matter how burdensome; my
heart belongs always to the poor blacks no matter how de-
praved and wicked they are in certain circumstances. I love
them, and if I could save them by giving my life, immediately,
I would be happy to do so.[178]

It is evident from his letters from Australia that he had a great
devotion to the Sacred Heart. The Passion of our Lord was his
favourite subject for meditation. To his ailing brother Jean-
Baptiste, back in Alsace, he had written, 'Take the cross as your
mantle, the crown of thorns of Our Saviour as your ear, the
lance, the whips and the nails for your blanket; lying down like
that you will sleep better. See! That's all I have read and learned
from books.'[179]

But Thiersé's own experience had taught him more. In 1866
he lay paralysed for some time with violent rheumatic pains:

I, who have such a struggle to pray, now pass the whole night in prayer, and I see, almost sensibly, Our Saviour carrying his cross on his bruised shoulders. I do not experience the night long. I pull myself from one side to the other, I am happy … I have forbidden the Daughters of Mary (Filles de Marie) to pray for my recovery. I have permitted them only to pray to the Good God to restore the use of my arm, to give me patience, a love of suffering and the strength to work, while at the same time leaving me my pains. Well, the good Sisters obtained that for me from the Good Lord. Oh, how I am obliged to recognise the goodness of God and the value of prayer. I can do my work, and joy fills my soul. I regard that as one of the greatest graces that God has given me. Thank the Good God for me and with me.[180]

Thiersé also expressed a lifelong devotion to Our Lady. In his writings he affectionately refers to Her as *La Bonne Mère* (The Good Mother). He had a special place in his heart for the Chapel of Our Lady of the Seven Dolours: 'It is my favoured place, especially in my troubles. How good it is to suffer at the feet of Mary whose heart was pierced by the seven swords. It sometimes seems to me that *La Bonne Mère* reproaches me, saying 'Take care that you are worthy of me.' I never leave that chapel without experiencing great relief and renewed strength.'[181]

Sometimes he suffered many purifying interior trials followed by great graces, which in some way absorbed all his faculties. On the occasion of his last annual retreat with his confrères in 1879, he describes the reviving effect of these exercises:

This year the Good Lord gave me the grace to be able to do my annual retreat with my confréres in Port Louis. I really thought I would miss it, because for eight days I was laid low with dysentery, which for three months – April, May and June-claimed many victims in Grand-Port. Fortunately, after three days I was able to overcome that deadly malady and followed all the exercises of the retreat. Those few days of recollection did my soul a world of good … I bless and thank the Good Lord and you, my Very Reverend Father, for obtaining that consolation at the end of my days.[182]

The Death of Father Thiersé

On 15 September 1879, Fr Corbet, the Provincial Superior, wrote that Thiersé had been very feeble for the last two weeks: 'He hardly eats, digestion is very difficult; he believes he is not far from the end.'[183] Two months later the ageing missionary described his own condition:

> I cannot be counted on anymore. I am hungry and thirsty, and I cannot eat or drink anything nourishing. No way can I swallow, no doubt my insides are not working. May the Good Lord be blessed for everything! I will what Our Saviour wills. I do not desire either life or health, nor relief from my suffering; only that the Good Lord in His mercy should take me to Him. I ask God's pardon, and yours, Very Reverend Father, and that of the whole Congregation for any faults of mine for the last 23 years. I thank all for the good that I have received in our Institute.[184]

According to newspaper accounts of his final days, Father Thiersé '...edified his numerous visitors by his patience and resignation, which touched the hearts of all.' In response to hopes that he would soon be well again, the priest replied, 'Alas, my son, my life is over: [he put his hand on his stomach] there is something there that cannot be healed. My affairs in this life are arranged; in a few days, in the other world, I will be rendering an account of my ministry.'[185]

On 11 May 1880, at 8.15 in the morning, Fr Thiersé breathed his last, gently, after very acute suffering.

At the special request of his parishioners of Grand-Port he was buried at their church in Mahebourg. In recognition of his devotion to them for a quarter of a century, his tomb bears the following epitaph:

Ci – git
F.J. Thiersé
Curé du Grand-Port
Vrai père des pauvres.
Il les evangelisa
Avec un zele infatigable

Leur fit eriger de nombreeux
Sanctuaires et ecoles,
Leur prodigua tous ses soins
dans leur soufrances.
Les paroissiens reconnaissants
Lui ont elevé ce monument.
1882

[Here lies F.J. Thiersé, parish priest of Grand-Port, a true father of the poor. He preached the Gospel to them with unflagging zeal, building numerous chapels and schools for them, and was lavish in his care for them in their sufferings. The grateful parishoners have built this memorial to him. 1882.]

The Church of the Holy Family, Albany
(From *The Record*, Perth, Western Australia; 4 October 1990)

Stained-glass windows recently installed in the church of the Holy Family symbolise the history of the Church in Albany since 1838, when the first Mass in Western Australia was celebrated at Mass Rock on the seaward side of the Port Authority building. [The windows were created through a bequest from Mr and Mrs Tom Adams.]

The top panel of the left window depicts the Southern Cross constellation, a sailing ship, a lighthouse and a whale, symbolising the origins of settlement in Albany. Beneath that, a stole with French tricolour calls to mind the French missionaries (1846-48) who laboured in the district among the Aborigines. Their mission hut is depicted in the next panel.

Below this is the crest of the Christian Brothers College, Albany, with its motto 'Deo Duce' – 'With God as Leader.'

Then comes a faithful rendition of the home of Lawrence Mooney, the father of the first Catholic family in Albany who offered hospitality to the French missionaries.

The site of their mission was discovered in 1960 when Fathers Noel Fitzsimons and Bernie Dwyer and Mr Roger Sounness excavated two mounds and found the remnants of the original fireplace, including a missionary's rosary and Dolour beads owned and used by the French missionaries at Santa Maria, Lake Mollyalup, near Mount Barker.[186]

There is now an annual Pilgrimage to Lake Mollyallup, the first Catholic Mission in the Southwest.

The top panel of the right window depicts the Holy Spirit. The Holy Family, patrons of the church, comprise the next panel, followed by a depiction of the original convent opened in

1878 by the Sisters of St Joseph of the Apparition. The crest of their school, St Joseph's, follows with its motto: 'Devotedness Unto Death.' The next panel depicts the first Catholic church built in Albany, *The Star of the Sea*, for the first parish priest, Father Aemélian Coll, OSB, in 1860.

Both window panels are decorated with flowers of the region-wattle, banksia, native wisteria-and a karri tree.

Assembly of Australia / Papua-New Guinea
(from *Spiritan News*, May 1997)

This meeting took place near Perth from 2-11 April 1997. The eight Holy Ghost Fathers from Papua-New Guinea as well as the 10 from Australia were present, including Kevin Conway, an Australian Lay Associate. Present also were the Superiors and representatives of the Provinces of origin as well as the Superior General, Father Pierre Schouver.

A two-day pilgrimage was led by Bishop Peter Quinn of Bunbury diocese '...in the steps of the missionaries of Libermann.' The Vicar General of Perth was present at the celebration in the Pro-Cathedral where Fr Bouchet's obsequies took place a few days after his arrival in Australia in 1846.

Father Schouver gave the following description:

I believe that the objectives of the Assembly were attained. But we received much more than we had foreseen. The whole Assembly was conscious of the great grace which was granted to us. We were really surprised by the wonderful welcome which that part of Australia gave us. They visited us, accompanied us, welcomed us into their homes during the weekend of the pilgrimage to Albany and Lake Mollyalup. The diocesan priests who had researched the archives and the original sites to reconstruct the history of Frs. Bouchet, Thévaux, and Thiersé and Brs Vincent and Théodore taught us our history. They invited us to take charge of the parish of Mount Barker where our predecessors had built their little mission.

An aboriginal, Maxime Fumagalli, recited her poem at the celebration:

> From far off places they had journeyed
> Those gentle servants of God
> They came and they suffered,
> But I've been waiting to greet you today
> In their spirit of commitment, I implore you to come
> To take up the challenge, of where they begun.

I had the impression that the Spirit of the Lord was trying to widen our vision: certainly in space, by bringing us from the other end of the world; also in time, by bringing us to retrace the footsteps of our confrères of 150 years ago; but also at a deeper level within ourselves, who are so much conditioned by our contemporary western value systems.

Contrary to appearances, the short adventure of Libermann's missionaries of a century and a half ago may not have been a failure after all. Maybe their suffering has been a source of life. Possibly their mission in Australia has not yet finished. Perhaps we have been called to begin to learn in their school.

Archival Sources

Annuaire de Diocèse. Diocése de Port-Louis, Mauritius, 1996.

Cabon, Adolphe, *Notes et Documents relatifs a la vie et l'oeuvre de Vénérable F.M.P., Libermann*. 13 Volumes. Paris, 1929-1956.

General News Bulletin. Archives of the Congregation of the Holy Spirit, Paris.

Littner, Henri, *L'aventure australienne de la Congrégation du Saint-Coeur-de Marie*. Paper presented in Rome to the General and his Council, Holy Ghost Fathers, 1980-1984.

Necrology of the Congregation of the Holy Spirit. Archives of the Congregation, Paris.

Spiritan Papers. No. 7, September-December, 1978 (Supplement to General Bulletin). Rome: Spiritan Studies Group.

Thévaux, F.M., *The Report of Father Francis M. Thévaux on the Mission of King George Sound (Albany) 1846-1848*. Trans. Mrs Bulbeck. Archives of the Congregation of the Holy Spirit, Paris.

Thévaux, Thiersé, Bouchet, *Letters From Cape Town*. Archives of the Congregation of the Holy Spirit, Paris.

The West Australian Catholic Record. June, 1974. Vol. 53, No. 1.

Other Sources

Allen, Maree G., *The Labourers' Friends: Sisters of Mercy in Victoria & Tasmania*. Melbourne: Hargreen Publishing Company, 1989.

Bourke, D.F., *The History of the Catholic Church in Western Australia*. Perth: Vanguard Service Print, 1979.

Briault, M., *La Reprise des missions d'Afrique au dix-neuvième siècle, Le Vénérable Père F.M.P. Libermann*. Paris: J. de Gigord, 1946.

Byrne, Geraldine, *Valiant Women*. Melbourne: Polding Press, 1981.

Condon, Kevin, *The Missionary College of All Hallows 1842-1891*. Dublin: All Hallows College, 1986.

Farragher, P.S., *Lead By the Spirit: The Life and Works of Claude Poulart des Place*. Paraclete Press, 1992.

Killerby, Catherine Kovesi, *Ursula Frayne*. South Fremantle: The University of Notre Dame Australia, 1996.

Lefebvre, F.A., *Trois prêtres boulonnais*. Bologne: Librarie de Mademoiselle Deligny, 1893.

Mamet, J., *Le Diocése de Port-Louis*. 1974.

McGough, W., *First Australian Adventure*. Irish Province Archives.

Michel, Joseph, *Le Pére Jacques Laval: Le Saint de l'Ile Maurice 1803-1864*. Paris: Editions Beauchesne, 1976.

Michel, Joseph, *Les auxiliaires laics du bienheureux Jacques Laval apotre de l'Ile Maurice*. Paris: Editions Beauchesne, 1988.

Moran, Cardinal Patrick Francis, *History of the Catholic Church in Australasia*. Sydney: Frank Coffee & Co., 1895.

Nagapen, Amédée, *Histoire de l'Eglise: Isle de France-Ile Maurice 1721-1968*. Port-Louis, Mauritius: Diocèse de Port-Louis, 1996.

Nagapen, Amédée, *La Naturalisation du Père J.D. Laval et des Missionaires Spiritains*. Port-Louis, Mauritius: Diocése de Port-Louis, 1992.

Roussel, Chanoine René, *Un Précurseur Monseigneur Luquet (1810-1858)*. Langres: Société Historique et Archéologique, 1960.

Salvado, Mgr Rudesindo, *Mémoires historiques sur l'Australie. French translation by L'Abbé Falcimagne*. Paris: Alphonse Pringuet, 1854.

Soltner, L., Barry, D., Cawley, M., and Forster, M.G., (trans). *Letters of Léandre Fonteinne*. Reprint from Guadalupo Abbey, Lafayette, Oregon (USA), 1984.

Vieira, Gérard, *Il Y A 150 Ans-Les Fils de Libermann*. Dakar: Imprimerie Saint-Paul, 1995.

Notes

The citation 'N.D.' refers to Adolphe Cabon, *Notes et Documents relatifs a la vie et l'oeuvre de Vénérable F.M.P. Libermann*. 13 Volumes. Paris, 1929-1956.

1   F. M. Thévaux, *The Report of Father Francis M. Thévaux on the Mission of King George Sound (Albany) 1846–1848*, trans. Mrs Bulbeck. Archives of the Congregation of the Holy Spirit, Paris, Box 134.

2   Le Vavasseur had with him in Bourbon Fathers Collin and Blanpin and was expecting the arrival of two Fathers and a Brother in April 1845. However, the situation in Bourbon was precarious for the Holy Heart of Mary missionaries, since the island was a French colony and therefore could be said to be under the jurisdiction of the Superior of the Holy Ghost Seminary, Paris. He had sole jurisdiction over the supply of priests for the colonies and so could bar entry to those not under his control. While the former Superior, Father Fourdinier, merely distrusted Libermann's priests, his successor, Father Leguay, elected in May 1845, was their declared enemy. The ministry of Father Le Vavasseur and his confrères to the black people was only tolerated because it was carried on outside the parish structure. Caution was prescribed!

3   Tisserant returned from Haiti with Fathers Stanislaus Arragon, Ernest Briot, Maurice Bouchet, Joseph Lossedot, and Brother Pierre Mersy.

4   The survivors were Father Jean-Remi Bessieux and Brother Gregoire Sey.
    The lesson of that disaster was that more preparatory work needed to be done. 'We rushed the matter, *a la missionaire*,' Libermann wrote to Emilie de Villeneuve, foundress of the Congregation of the Immaculate Conception of Castres, on 23 July 1845 (N.D. VII, p. 245), 'and we were torn to pieces.' Guinea would always be the special mission field of predilection for the young Institute. 'We suffered a lot there... I shall never abandon Guinea, unless it cannot be avoided,' he often repeated. (Libermann to Bessieux, 4 May 1845.)
    To explore the situation, in June 1845 Libermann sent out to Goree Fathers Arragon and Briot as well as Brother Pierre Mersy, who had all come back from Haiti six weeks earlier. But Goree, a tiny island (1,000 by 450 yards) less than two miles off the mainland, was part

of the colony of Senegal and therefore within the jurisdiction of the colonial clergy. Moreover, half the island was occupied by the French navy and the remainder crowded with some 5,000 people. There were schools for boys and girls, a convent of the Sisters of St Joseph of Cluny (founded in 1819), a hospital, and a church staffed by three native-born colonial priests (Father Moussa, Father Boilat, Vice-Prefect Apostolic at St. Louis, and Father Fridoil).

Before leaving Paris, Fathers Arragon and Briot and Brother Mersy made a courtesy call on Father Leguay, Superior of the Holy Ghost Seminary, who told them he was not in a position to delegate any jurisdiction to them. But he was happy to entrust them with a letter to the Vice-Prefect Apostolic, L'Abbé Boilet, in which he forbade Boilet to grant them any jurisdiction at all!

Their reception in Senegal was rather cool. And when they landed on Goree July 26, the local priest was none too pleased. 'This evening at 7 p.m.,' wrote L'Abbé Boilet, 'I received a letter from L'Abbé Moussa, Parish Priest of Goree, saying that a local notable Jean Dupuy arrived with the Director of the Libermann missionaries. This gentleman arrived at 10 pm. I waited for him even up to 11 pm. Instead of presenting himself to the Parish Priest of St Louis he settled in with the Brothers of Christian Doctrine without as much as bidding me 'Good Night.' Initial impoliteness. We will see what happens next... We all think it our duty to protest against the Libermann missionaries who have sought to exercise the sacred ministry in the colony, without the permission of the Holy Ghost Fathers.' (Gérard Vieira, *Il Y A 150 Ans-Les Fils de Libermann* (Dakar: Imprimerie Saint-Paul, 1995), p. 30.)

Moreover, as the exact limits of the prefecture-apostolic of Senegal were not clear, one did not know where the Vicariate of the Two Guineas began. No wonder misunderstandings arose. Eventually, however, a compromise was reached: Libermann's men moved to Dakar on the neighbouring peninsula. A tract of three hectares of land was bought on the site where the town hall stands today, and so the church in Dakar was born. It had the advantage that they would not be under the French Government and not subject to the Vicar Apostolic of Senegal.

From there the Mission of Dakar took off, but not without the Cross. Eugene Tisserant was appointed Prefect Apostolic of the two Guineas in October 1845. On his way there he lost his life in a shipwreck off the coast of Morocco on 7 December 1845. His successor, Mgr Truffet, arrived in March 1847 but died in November of the same year.

5   Letter to Mother Javouhey (foundress of the Sisters of St Joseph of Cluny), N.D. VII, p. 830.
6   Letter to the Goree Community, 18 August 1845; N.D. VII, p. 274f.
7   *Ibid.*, p. 404.

8   Letter to Arragon, 8 May 1846; N.D. VIII, p. 146.

9   Letter to the Community of Bourbon, 6 September 1845; N.D. VII, p. 294.

10 Letter to Arragon, 8 May 1846; N.D. VIII, p. 145f.

11 Henri Littner, *L'aventure australienne de la Congrégation du Saint-Coeur-de-Marie*, paper presented in Rome, to the General and his Council, Holy Ghost Fathers, 1980-1984, Ms. p. 7.

12 P.S. Farragher, *Lead By the Spirit: The Life and Works of Claude Poulart des Place* (Paraclete Press, 1992), p. 260. Brady first entered a junior seminary in Paris opened
    1 October 1824 by Fr Jacques Bertout, 6th Superior General of the Holy Ghost Fathers. On the roll of the junior seminarians (ages 15-16) appear the names of three Cavan boys: Richard Smith, future Archbishop of Trinidad; Philip O'Reilly; and John Brady, later Bishop of Perth.

13 Littner, p. 9.

14 D.F. Bourke, *The History of the Catholic Church in Western Australia* (Perth: Vanguard Service Print, 1979), p. 6.

15 *Ibid.*, p. 14.

16 Patrick Francis Cardinal Moran, *History of the Catholic Church in Australasia* (Sydney: Frank Coffee & Co., 1895), p. 554.

17 *Ibid.*, p. 356.

18 It was said to have been a primitive structure, 60 by 24 feet. The four walls were built first and then openings were made for the doors and windows. Subsequently, buttresses had to be added to support the tottering walls! In June 1844, Archbishop Polding received a letter from Fr Joostens stating that the mission was going well, that a church to hold 150 people had been erected, and that he had 20 to 30 children attending school.

19 Bishop Polding, on an official visit to Rome in 1842, had already recommended a separate ecclesiastical entity for Perth, to be supported financially by the Society of the Propagation of Faith. (Chanoine René Roussel, *Un Précurseur Monseigneur Luquet (1810-1858)* (Langres: Société Historique et Archéologique, 1960), p. 80.)

20 Cardinal Moran, p. 557. In a second letter dated 21 November 1844, Brady added that the Archbishop of Sydney would prefer French or Belgian priests for the native missions, and suggested Ullathorne as bishop. But Ullathorne declined for health reasons, having worked for 10 years among the colonists and convicts. Ullathorne's pamphlet, 'Horrors of Transportation,' is regarded as a classic condemnation of the system. In 1850 he became the first Bishop of Birmingham, England.

21 From an unsigned note in the hand of Father Thiersé, one of Libermann's young priests who would join Brady's expedition to Australia. (Littner, p. 10)

22 Littner, p. 11.

23 Before departing, Serra and Salvado had a special audience with

Pope Gregory XVI, himself a Benedictine. In 1840 he had published *'Probe Nostris'* on the missionary apostolate, thus making the nineteenth century 'the mission century.' In view of their subsequent careers, his advice to them was significant:

Be mindful of the example set you by those apostolic men, our brethren, who of old not only converted to the faith so many nations and peoples, but likewise instructed them in the ways of civilisation and the arts of cultural life, and remember you are entering a work like theirs.

(Moran, p. 563)

24 Cardinal Moran, p. 559.

25 Hand's visit came at a critical moment for Libermann: Father Jacques Laval had been dispatched in 1841 to the island of Mauritius, Indian Ocean, a former French colony and since 1814 British. After Laval, no more French missionaries had been admitted. Libermann strongly urged Hand to do for the blacks in the English colonies what he himself was doing for those in the French colonies. At any moment he expected a request to supply priests for Mauritius. Hand promised to do his best but could not oblige as his college was not yet open. (N.D. III, p. 18.)

Two months later, on 30 July 1842, Libermann wrote to Hand in response to an urgent request from (Vicar Apostolic of Mauritius) Bishop Collier for two priests. He asked Hand to seek out two English or Irish priests, with some knowledge of French, who would be willing to join his little society in the work for the blacks. He assured Hand that he would take care that the new recruits '...were not imbued with the national jealousy so common between the French and the English!' Moreover, *'...If a foundation was made in Mauritius it could be the beginning of this work for you.'* Indeed, after its foundation on 1 November 1842, All Hallows did send many priests to serve in Mauritius as diocesan priests, including Fathers Christopher Conway, Denis Spellissy, and Andrew McGovern. Between 1826 and 1972, 62 Irish diocesan priests served in Mauritius. (Amédée Nagapen, *La Naturalisation du Père J.D. Laval et des Missionaires Spiritains* (Port-Louis, Mauritius: Diocése de Port Louis, 1992), pp. 139-140.)

26 Letter to Arragon, 8 May 1846; N.D. VIII, p. 146.

27 N.D. VII, p. 501f.

28 Littner, p. 15.

29 N.D. VII, p. 318.

30 N.D. IX, p. 76 and p. 184.

31 N.D. VIII, p. 47.

32 *Ibid.*, p. 249.

33 N.D. VII, p. 249.

34 Littner, p. 17.

35 N.D. VIII, p. 47f.

36 Littner, p. 17.

37 Littner, p. 18.

38 *Ibid.*
39 N.D. XIII, Appendix, p. 47 and pp. 83-84.
40 C.S.Sp. Necrology, Tome 1, p. 614.
41 *Ibid.*, p. 615.
42 Lettres Spirituelles du R.P. Libermann, Tome 11, p. 342.
43 Letter to Father Briot, 28 October 1845; N.D. VII, p. 349.
44 C.S.Sp. Necrology, Tome 1, p. 18.
45 N.D. VII, p. 307f. Eusébe had to go to England to escape conscription, met our brothers there and left with them. His first vows were made on arrival at Perth, February 1846. In 1848 he became novice master and model to a brothers' noviciate established by Fr Collin in Réunion Island, Indian Ocean. He moved to the Island of Guadeloupe in the West Indies towards the end of 1853 and there withdrew from the Congregation in 1857.
46 Littner, p. 20.
47 Maree G. Allen, *The Labourers' Friends: Sisters of Mercy in Victoria and Tasmania* (Melbourne: Hargreen Publishing Co., 1989), p. 8.
48 Catherine Kovesi Killerby, Ursula Frayne (South Fremantle: The University of Notre Dame Australia, 1996), p. 101.
49 *Ibid.*, p. 103.
50 *Ibid.*
51 Geraldine Byrne, *Valiant Women* (Melbourne: Polding Press, 1981), p. 15.
52 Killerby, p. 106.
53 L. Soltner and others (trans.), *Letters of Léandre Fonteinne*, p. 87.
54 *Ibid.*
55 Thévaux's letter to Libermann from the Cape of Good Hope, p. 5. C.S.Sp. Archives, Paris, Box 134 V.
56 Thiersé's letter to his mother, 8 February 1846, C.S.Sp. Archives, Paris, Box 134 V.
57 Littner, p. 26.
58 Byrne, p.16.
59 Thévaux's letter to Libermann from Capetown, 22 October 1845, p. 10.
60 Letter from Thiersé, February 1846, C.S.Sp. Archives, Paris.
61 Thévaux, letter of 10 January 1846.
62 Thiersé in a letter to his parish priest, 4 February 1846.
63 Byrne, Sister Ursula, Letter 5, p. 19.
64 Thévaux letter, 31 January 1846.
65 Mgr. Rudesindo Salvado, *Mémoires historiques sur l'Australie* (Paris: Alphonse Pringuet, 1854).
66 Killerby, p. 113.
67 Bourke, p.12.
68 Killerby, p. 114.
69 *Ibid.*, p.113.
70 Thévaux's letter to Libermann, 31 January 1846, C.S.Sp. Archives, Paris.

71 *Ibid.*

72 The precise location of Father Bouchet's grave was unknown until July 2000. The approximate location was long believed to be close to St John's Pro-Cathedral, the first Catholic church in Western Australia, which is today on the grounds of Mercedes College in Perth. Thanks to the efforts of diocesan archivist Sister Frances Stibi PBVM and the generous technical assistance of Mr Ralph Newton of Western Geotechnics of Perth, this company's surface-penetrating radar confirmed the presence of two graves just a few metres south of the southern wall of St John's. Analysis of this radar scan strongly suggests that metallic objects in one of the graves identifies it as that of Father Bouchet, who is known to have been buried in full habit (likely including Rosary beads and / or a crucifix). The second grave is believed to be that of Irish catechist John O'Reilly, who died of cholera some 13 months after Father Bouchet.

73 Byrne, p. 24.

74 Killerby, p. 117.

75 Thévaux's letter to Libermann, 23 July 1847, C.S.Sp. Archives, Paris.

76 Bourke, p. 15.

77 *Ibid.*

78 Thévaux's letter to Libermann from Perth, 31 January 1846.

79 *Ibid.*, p. 6.

80 31 January 1846, p. 7.

81 *Ibid.*, p. 7.

82 Littner, p. 34.

83 Bourke, p. 30.

84 Moran, p. 565.

85 Madden's letter to Dr Meagher, Vicar General of Dublin Diocese. (Moran, p. 565.) The Anglican Archdeacon paid this tribute to Dr Madden: 'Dr Madden turns out excellent, although Roman Catholic. One great thing is that he is determined to judge for himself, not to be swayed by interested parties.' (Bourke, p. 33.)

86 Thévaux's Report, p. 3.

87 *Ibid.*, p. 4.

88 *Ibid.*, p. 6.

89 Thiersé, 8 February 1846, C.S.Sp. Archives, Paris.

90 Thévaux's Report, p. 7.

91 Littner, p. 38. Letter, 14 February 1846.

92 Thévaux's Report, p. 7.

93 *Ibid.*, p. 9.

94 *Ibid.*, p. 13.

95 *Ibid.*, p. 39.

96 Thévaux's letter to Libermann, 25 March 1846.

97 Thévaux's Report, p. 14.

98 Littner, p. 45.

99 Thévaux's Report, p. 33, 28 August 1846.

100 Thévaux's Report, p. 35, 3 September 1846.
101 Littner, p. 47.
102 Thévaux's Report, p. 39.
103 *Ibid.*, p. 46.
104 The French fathers' mission site at Mollyalup was not discovered until 1960. See note 186 below.
105 According to a letter (almost certainly from Signor Caporelli), Brady had received 24,000 francs, but there is some confusion about the precise amount. According to Notes and Documents, Vol. IX, p. 73, Bishop Brady's mission should have received 49,600 francs. Why the discrepancy? It seems certain that Brady retained 25,600 to pay his debts; the remaining 24,000 francs would have been allotted as follows: 6,000 for the sisters, 5,000 for the Benedictines, and 3,000 for the Sound, leaving 10,000 unaccounted for. Apparently the Propagation of the Faith, having learned that the actual population (including natives) numbered less than Brady had claimed, insisted on a more realistic accounting.
106 Thévaux's Report, p. 55.
107 *Ibid.*, p. 60.
108 *Ibid.*, p. 64.
109 *Ibid.*, p. 65.
110 Littner, p. 54.
111 Ibid.
112 N.D. IX, pp. 55-56.
113 Littner, p. 38.
114 N.D. IX, pp. 74-76.
115 *Ibid.*
116 N.D. IX, pp. 138-141.
117 Thévaux's letter to Libermann, June 1847.
118 *Ibid.*
119 Thévaux's Report, p. 69.
120 Libermann's letter to Thévaux, 27 February 1848; N.D. X, p. 93.
121 Brady's letters to Libermann, 19 August 1847.
122 Littner, p. 62.
123 *Ibid.*, p. 63.
124 N.D. X, pp. 248-249.
125 Libermann's letter to Le Vavasseur, 14 October 1847; N.D. IX, p. 284.
126 N.D. X, p. 93f.
127 Littner, p. 66.
128 Ibid.
129 Ibid.
130 Thiersé file, C.S.Sp. Archives, Paris.
131 Littner, p. 67.
132 Thiersé's letter to Libermann, 14 June 1848. C.S.Sp. Archives, Paris.
133 Littner, p. 69.
134 General Bulletin – C.S.Sp. Necrology, Vol. I, p. 17.

135 Bourke, p. 34.

136 Letter to Cardinal Cullen of Dublin, 18 December 1871; Diocesan Archives, Clonliffe; Box 130.

137 Bourke, p. 51, footnote 66. *Acta Sac. Cong. De Prop. Fide;* Vol. 213.974.

138 Libermann's letter to Cardinal Fransoni, 9 April 1848.

139 Libermann's letter of 27 February 1847; N.D. X, pp. 94-95.

140 Libermann's letter of 19 February 1849; N.D. XI, p. 44.

141 Thiersé's letter to Libermann; Littner, p. 72.

142 Joseph Michel, *Le Père Jacques Laval: Le Saint de l'Ile Maurice 1803-1864* (Paris: Editions Beauchesne, 1976), p. 165. [Father Laval was beatified in Rome, 29 April 1979.]

143 C.S.Sp. Necrology – Notice sur le P. Thévaux, p. 617.

144 Report to Propaganda by Father Joseph O'Dwyer in Michel, p. 268. Amédée Nagapen, *Histoire de l'Eglise: Isle de France – Ile Maurice 1721-1968* (Port-Louis, Mauritius: Diocèse de Port-Louis, 1996), p. 127f.

145 Thévaux's letter to Libermann, 6 December 1847.

146 Thévaux's letter to Libermann, January 1848.

147 Nagapen, *Histoire*, p. 119.

148 C.S.Sp. Necrology – Notice sur le P. Thévaux, p. 168.

149 *Spiritan Papers* No. 7 (September-December, 1978; Supplement to General Bulletin. Rome: Spiritan Studies Group), p. 53.

150 C.S.Sp. Necrology- Notice sur le P. Thévaux, p. 620. Letter of Fr Guilmin, 16 April 1867.

151 Thévaux's letter to Schwindenhammer of 6 July 1860. *Ibid.*, p. 620.

152 Thévaux's letter of 3 May 1872. *Ibid.*, p. 621.

153 *Ibid.*, p. 622.

154 Letter of Father Gilloux to the Superior General. *Ibid.*, p. 624.

155 Report in the local papers, *Le Pays, Le Cerneen, L'Univers*, 1877.

156 C.S.Sp. Necrology – Notice sur le P. Thiersé, p. 24.

157 Laval's letter to Schwindenhammer, 23 September 1856. C.S.Sp. Archives, Paris.

158 Nagapen, *Histoire*, p. 132.

159 C.S.Sp. Necrology – Notice sur le P. Thiersé, p. 24.

160 Thiersé's letter to the Superior General, 23 April 1852. *Ibid.*

161 *Ibid.*, p. 25.

162 Thiersé's letter to his brother, 30 September 1852. *Ibid.*, p. 26.

163 *Ibid.*, p. 27.

164 Gomm's Dispatch of 26 September 1846. Nagapen, *La Naturalisation*, p. 25.

165 *Ibid.*, p. 41.

166 Michel, p. 199.

167 A strange incident took place in 1860 (after Thiersé had returned to Mauritius) during a Corpus Christi religious procession in Mahebourg: it was reported that a British cavalry officer, one 'Quarter Master Drake,' somehow rode his horse into the crowd.

Thiersé promptly '...did give the horse of the Quarter Master a stroke of his parasol.' Through Bishop Collier, Thiersé sent an apology: 'I beg to offer the expression of my regret for having struck your horse at the procession of the *Fête-Dieu*, though I did so to prevent some serious accident which I apprehended would otherwise occur.' Quartermaster Drake refused this apology, and Thiersé – even at request of the Bishop – declined to make any further expression of regret. Nagapen, *La Naturalisation*, p. 75f.

168 C.S.Sp. Necrology – Notice sur le P. Thiersé, p. 27.

169 *Ibid.*, p. 28.

170 Thiersé's letter of 22 December 1855. *Ibid.*, p. 28.

171 *Ibid.*, p. 29.

172 Thiersé's letter of 7 January 1850.

173 Thiersé's letter from Grand-Port, 28 May 1872. *Ibid.*, p. 31.

174 *Le Pays, Le Cerneen*, etc. *Ibid.*, p. 32.

175 C.S.Sp. Necrology, Tome 1, pp. 36-38.

176 Thévaux's Report, p. 35.

177 Thiersé's letters of 13 May 1854 and 6 January 1875. *Ibid.*, p. 36.

178 Thiersé's letter of 23 August 1870. *Ibid.*, p. 37.

179 Thiersé's letter of September 1852. *Ibid.*, p. 38.

180 Thiersé's letter of 4 May 1866. *Ibid.*

181. *Ibid.*, p. 39.

182. *Ibid.*, p. 39.

183. *Ibid.*, p. 40.

184 Thiersé's letter to Father Corbet, November 1879. *Ibid.*, p. 40.

185 As reported in the local paper, *Le Pays*, 19 May 1880. *Ibid.*, p. 41.

186 On 28 March 1960 Fathers Dwyer and Fitzsimons went to try and find the location of the Mission House. Mr Sounness, whom they had interested in their venture, made some inquiries among the oldest inhabitants of the area and was able to show them what was commonly believed to be the location. Two small mounds of stone marked the site. One of these turned out to be the fireplace, whose foundations they unearthed about 12 inches below the present ground level. In the ashes of this fireplace, two beads were found. On the reverse side of the metal crucifix attached to the large beads is stamped the figure of Our Lady, and the words: 'Mère de Dieu, Priez pour Nous' (Mother of God, pray for us). (Text of an illuminated scroll presented to Father Pierre Schouver, Superior General of the Congregation of the Holy Spirit and the Holy Heart of Mary, April 1991, Oceania Assembly, Perth.)